HARRAP'S

French

PHRASE BOOK

Compiled by
LEXUS

HARRAP
London   Paris

First published in Great Britain 1988
by HARRAP BOOKS Ltd
Chelsea House, 26 Market Square, Bromley, Kent BR1 1NA

© *Harrap Books Ltd/Lexus Ltd* 1988

ISBN 0245-54661-8
In the United States, ISBN 0-13-383175-2

Reprinted 1988, 1989 (*three times*), 1990, (*twice*)

Library of Congress Cataloging-in-Publication Data

Harrap's French phrase book/compiled by Lexus.
p.   cm.
English and French.
"First published in Great Britain, 1988" – T.p. verso.
ISBN 0-13-383175-2 (Prentice Hall)
1. French language – Conversation and phrase books – English.
I. Lexus (Firm)
PC2121.H24 1990   89-48975
448.3′421 – dc20 – dc20   CIP

Printed in England by Clays Ltd, St Ives plc

CONTENTS

INTRODUCTION	5
PRONUNCIATION	6
GENERAL PHRASES	7
COMING AND GOING	11
GETTING A ROOM	14
EATING OUT	17
MENU READER	19
HAVING A DRINK	25
COLLOQUIAL EXPRESSIONS	27
GETTING AROUND	29
SHOPPING	33
FRANCE AND THINGS FRENCH	35
MONEY	36
ENTERTAINMENT	38
THE BEACH	40
PROBLEMS	42
HEALTH	45
SPORT	47
THE POST OFFICE	48
TELEPHONING	49
The Alphabet	51
NUMBERS, THE DATE, THE TIME	52
ENGLISH-FRENCH DICTIONARY	55
FRENCH-ENGLISH DICTIONARY	89
GRAMMAR	121
CONVERSION TABLES	128

The phrase sections in this new book are concise and to the point. In each section you will find: a list of basic vocabulary; a selection of useful phrases; a list of common words and expressions that you will see on signs and notices. A full pronunciation guide is given for things you'll want to say or ask and typical replies to some of your questions are listed.

Of course, there are bound to be occasions when you want to know more. So this book allows for this by containing a two way French-English dictionary with a total of some 5,000 references. This will enable you to build up your French vocabulary, to make variations on the phrases in the phrase sections and to recognize more of the French words that you will see or hear when travelling about.

As well as this we have given a menu reader covering about 200 dishes and types of food — so that you will know what you are ordering! And, as a special feature, there is a section on colloquial French.

Speaking the language can make all the difference to your trip. So:

bonne chance !
bon shonss
good luck!

and

bon voyage !
boN vwoy-ahj
have a good trip!

5

PRONUNCIATION

In the phrase sections of this book a pronunciation guide has been given by writing the French words as though they were English. So if you read out the pronunciation as English words a French person should be able to understand you. Some notes on this:

*a*N a typical French nasal sound; do not actually pronounce the 'n'; for example, in the word 'vin' speak the pronunciation guide 'vaN' as though you were saying the English word 'van' — but stop short of saying the 'n'.

*o*N the same applies to this nasal sound; for example, when saying 'bonjour' — which is written as 'boN-joor' — go to pronounce 'bon' but cut off the 'n'.

ew as in 'pew' or 'few'

uh similar to the 'e' sound in 'the' or 'other'

j pronounce this like the 's' in 'treasure' or the 'z' in 'seizure'

GENERAL PHRASES

hello
bonjour; (*evening*) bonsoir
bon-joor; bon-swahr

hi
salut
sa-lew

good morning
bonjour
bon-joor

good evening
bonsoir
bon-swahr

good night
bonne nuit
bon nwee

pleased to meet you
enchanté
on-shontay

goodbye
au revoir
or-vwahr

cheerio
salut
sa-lew

see you
à bientôt
ah byanto

yes
oui
wee

GENERAL PHRASES

no
non
non

yes please
oui, volontiers
wee volont-yay

no thank you
non merci
non mairsee

please
s'il vous plaît
seelvooplay

thank you/ thanks
merci
mairsee

thanks very much
merci beaucoup
mairsee bo-koo

you're welcome
il n'y a pas de quoi
eel nya pa duh kwa

sorry
excusez-moi
eks-kewzay mwa

sorry? (*didn't understand*)
comment ?
komon

how are you?
comment allez-vous ?
komon talay-voo

very well, thank you
très bien merci
tray byan mairsee

and yourself?
et vous-même ?
ay voo-mem

GENERAL PHRASES

excuse me *(to get attention)*
pardon, Monsieur/ Madame
pardoN, muh-syuh/ madam

how much is it?
combien est-ce que ça coûte?
koNbyaN eskuh sa koot

can I ...?
je peux ... ?
juh puh

can I have ...?
je voudrais ...
juh voodray

I'd like to ...
j'aimerais ...
jemray

where is ...?
où est ... ?
oo ay

it's not ...
ce n'est pas ...
suh nay pa

is it ...?
c'est ... ?
say

is there ... here?
y a-t-il ... ici ?
yateel ... eesee

could you say that again?
pourriez-vous répéter ?
poor-yay-voo ray-pay-tay

please don't speak so fast
pourriez-vous parler plus lentement ?
poor-yay-voo parlay plew loN-tmoN

I don't understand
je ne comprends pas
juh nuh koNproN pa

GENERAL PHRASES

OK
d'accord
dakor

that's OK (*don't worry etc*)
ça va
sa va

come on, let's go!
allons-y !
aloN-zee

wait for me!
attendez-moi !
atoNday-mwa

what's that in French?
comment ça s'appelle en français ?
komoN sa sapel oN froNsay

that's fine!
ça va très bien
sa va tray byaN

accès interdit	no entry
à vendre	for sale
dames	ladies
défense d'afficher	stick no bills
entrée libre	admission free
fermé	closed
interdit	forbidden
messieurs	gents
ne pas . . .	do not . . .
ouvert	open
papiers	litter
peinture fraîche	wet paint
poussez	push
prière de . . .	please . . .
tirez	pull
veuillez . . .	please . . .

COMING AND GOING

airport	l'aéroport *m airopor*
baggage	les bagages *mpl bagahj*
book	réserver *rayzairvay*
(*in advance*)	
coach	un car *kar*
docks	les docks *mpl dok*
ferry	le ferry *fairree*
gate	la porte *port*
(*at airport*)	
harbour	le port *por*
hovercraft	l'aéroglisseur *m airogleesur*
plane	l'avion *m avyoɴ*
sleeper	une couchette *kooshet*
station	la gare *gar*
taxi	un taxi *taxee*
terminal	le terminal *tairmeenahl*
train	le train *traɴ*

a ticket to . . .
un billet pour . . .
aɴ beeyay poor

I'd like to reserve a seat
j'aimerais réserver une place
jemray rayzairvay ewn plass

smoking/ non-smoking please
fumeurs/ non fumeurs, s'il vous plaît
fewmur/ ɴoɴ fewmur seelvooplay

a window seat please
près de la fenêtre, s'il vous plaît
pray duh la fuhnaitr seelvooplay

which platform is it for . . .?
de quel quai part le train pour . . . ?
duh kel kay par luh traɴ poor

COMING AND GOING

what time is the next flight?
à quelle heure part le prochain vol ?
ah kel ur par luh proshan vol

is this the right train for ...?
c'est bien le train pour ... ?
say byan luh tran poor

is this bus going to ...?
cet autobus va-t-il à ... ?
set otobewss vateel ah

is this seat free?
cette place est libre ?
set plass ay leebr

do I have to change (trains)?
est-ce que je dois changer (de train) ?
eskuh juh dwa shonjay (duh tran)

is this the right stop for ...?
c'est bien cet arrêt pour ... ?
say byan set aray poor

which terminal is it for ...?
quel terminal pour ... ?
kel tairmeenahl poor

is this ticket OK?
ce billet va bien ?
suh beeyay va byan

I want to change my ticket
je voudrais changer mon billet
juh voodray shonjay mon beeyay

thanks for a lovely stay
merci pour votre hospitalité
mairsee poor votr ospeetaleetay

thanks very much for coming to meet me
c'est vraiment gentil d'être venu me chercher
say vraymon jontee daitr vuhnew muh shairshay

well, here we are in ...
nous voici donc à ...
noo vwasee donk ah

rien à déclarer ?
ree-aN ah day-klaray
anything to declare?

ouvrez votre valise, s'il vous plaît
oovray votr valeez seelvooplay
would you mind opening this bag please?

arrivée	arrivals
attachez vos ceintures	fasten your seat belts
bagages à main	hand luggage
billets	tickets
compostez votre billet	stamp your ticket in the machine
contrôle des passeports	passport control
correspondance	connection
départ	departures
douane	customs
embarquement immédiat	boarding now
enregistrement des bagages	check-in
entrée	entrance
fumeurs	smoking
gare (SNCF)	railway station
grandes lignes	main lines
navette	shuttle service
non fumeurs	no smoking
porte	gate
quai	platform
RER	fast limited-stop metro in Paris
réservation obligatoire	booking essential
retrait des bagages	baggage claim
retard	delay
salle d'attente	waiting room
sortie	exit
tenez la droite	keep right

GETTING A ROOM

balcony	un balcon	*balkoN*
bed	un lit	*lee*
breakfast	le petit déjeuner	*ptee dayjurnay*
dining room	la salle à manger	*salamoNjay*
dinner	le dîner	*deenay*
double room	une chambre pour deux	*shoNbr poor duh*
guesthouse	la pension	*poNsyoN*
hotel	un hôtel	*otel*
key	la clé	*klay*
lunch	le déjeuner	*dayjurnay*
night	une nuit	*nwee*
private bathroom	une salle de bain particulière	*sal duh baN parteekewl-yair*
reception	la réception	*raysepssyoN*
room	une chambre	*shoNbr*
shower	une douche	*doosh*
single room	une chambre pour une personne	*shoNbr poor ewn pairson*
with bath	avec salle de bain	*avek sal duh baN*
youth hostel	une auberge de jeunesse	*obairj duh jurness*

do you have a room for one night?
vous avez une chambre pour une nuit ?
voo zavay ewn shoNbr poor ewn nwee

do you have a room for one person?
vous avez une chambre pour une personne ?
voo zavay ewn shoNbr poor ewn pairson

do you have a room for two people?
vous avez une chambre pour deux personnes ?
voo zavay ewn shoNbr poor duh pairson

we'd like to rent a room for a week
nous aimerions louer une chambre pour une semaine
noo zemree-oN looay ewn shoNbr poor ewn suhmen

14

GETTING A ROOM

I'm looking for a good, cheap room
je cherche une bonne chambre pas chère
juh shairsh ewn bon shoɴbr kee nuh swa pa shair

I have a reservation
j'ai réservé
jay rayzairvay

how much is it?
quel est le prix de la chambre ?
kel ay luh pree duh la shoɴbr

can I see the room please?
est-ce que je peux voir la chambre, s'il vous plaît ?
eskuh juh puh vwahr la shoɴbr seelvooplay

does that include breakfast?
est-ce que le petit déjeuner est inclus dans le prix ?
eskuh luh ptee dayjurnay ay taɴklew doɴ luh pree

a room overlooking the sea
une chambre avec vue sur la mer
ewn shoɴbr avek vew sewr la mair

we'd like to stay another night
nous aimerions rester encore une nuit
noo zemree-oɴ restay oɴkor ewn nwee

we will be arriving late
nous arriverons tard le soir
noo zareevroɴ tar luh swahr

can I have my bill please?
pourriez-vous préparer ma note, s'il vous plaît ?
pooryay-voo prayparay ma not seelvooplay

I'll pay cash
je vais payer comptant
juh vay payay koɴtoɴ

can I pay by credit card?
vous acceptez les cartes de crédit ?
voo zakseptay lay kart duh kraydee

will you give me a call at 6.30 in the morning?
pouvez-vous me réveiller à 6 heures 30 demain matin ?
poovay-voo muh rayvay-yay ah see zur troɴt duhmaɴ mataɴ

GETTING A ROOM

at what time do you serve breakfast/ dinner?
à quelle heure servez-vous le petit déjeuner/ dîner ?
ah kel ur sairvay-voo luh ptee dayjurnay/ deenay

can we have breakfast in our room?
est-ce que nous pouvons prendre le petit déjeuner dans
notre chambre ?
eskuh noo poovon prondr luh ptee dayjurnay don notr shonbr

thanks for putting us up
merci de nous avoir hébergé
mairsee duh noo zavwahr aybairjay

ascenseur	lift
auberge de jeunesse	youth hostel
chambres à louer	rooms to rent
complet	no vacancies
demi-pension	half board
douche	shower
étage	floor
issue de secours	fire escape
parking réservé aux clients de l'hôtel	car park for hotel residents only
pension	guesthouse
prière de ne pas déranger	please do not disturb
rez-de-chaussée	ground floor
salle à manger	dining room
salle de bain	bathroom
sous-sol	basement
veuillez libérer votre chambre avant midi	please vacate your room by 12 noon
1er étage	first floor
2ème étage	second floor

EATING OUT

bill	l'addition *f adeessyon*
dessert	le dessert *desair*
drink	boire *bwahr*
eat	manger *monjay*
food	la nourriture *nooreetewr*
main course	le plat principal *pla pranseepal*
menu	le menu *muhnew*
restaurant	le restaurant *restoron*
salad	une salade *salahd*
service	le service *sairveess*
starter	l'entrée *f ontray*
tip	le pourboire *poorbwahr*
waiter	le garçon *garson*
waitress	la serveuse *sairvurz*

a table for three, please
une table pour trois, s'il vous plaît
ewn tabl poor trwa seelvooplay

can I see the menu?
j'aimerais voir le menu
jemray vwahr luh muhnew

we'd like to order
nous aimerions commander
noo zemree-on komonday

what do you recommend?
qu'est-ce que vous recommandez ?
keskuh voo ruhkomonday

I'd like ... please
j'aimerais ..., s'il vous plaît
jemray ... seelvooplay

waiter!
garçon !
garson

EATING OUT

waitress!
Mademoiselle !
madmwazel

could we have the bill, please?
l'addition, s'il vous plaît
ladeessyon seelvooplay

two white coffees please
deux crèmes, s'il vous plaît
duh krem seelvooplay

that's for me
c'est pour moi
say poor mwa

some more bread please
encore un peu de pain, s'il vous plaît
onkor an puh duh pan seelvooplay

a bottle of red/white wine please
une bouteille de vin rouge/blanc, s'il vous plaît
ewn bootay duh van rooj/blon seelvooplay

auberge	inn
brasserie	café serving food
dames	ladies
grill	restaurant serving grilled meat
menu à 60 F	set menu costing 60 francs
messieurs	gents
plat du jour	today's set menu
plats à emporter	take-away meals
restaurant nord-africain	North African restaurant
service (non) compris	service charge (not) included
snack	snack bar

à la bordelaise with red wine and shallots
à la provençale with tomatoes, garlic and herbs
à point medium
ail garlic
amande almond
anchois anchovies
andouillette small sausage
anguille eel
artichaut artichoke
assiette de charcuterie selection of cold meats and pâté
avocat vinaigrette avocado with French dressing

bavette à l'échalote grilled beef with shallots
beignet fritter, doughnut
betterave beetroot
bien cuit well done (*meat*)
bifteck steak
bisque seafood soup
blanquette de veau veal stew
bleu very rare
boeuf bourguignon beef cooked in red wine
boeuf mode beef stew with carrots
bouchée à la reine vol au vent
boudin black pudding
bouillabaisse fish soup from the South of France
boulette meatball
braisé braised
brochette kebab
brugnon nectarine

cabillaud cod
caille quail
calmar squid
canard à l'orange duck in orange sauce
canard laqué Peking duck
caneton aux cerises duckling with cherries

MENU READER

carbonnade beef stew in beer
carottes Vichy carrots in butter and parsley
cassis blackcurrant
cassoulet casserole with pork, sausages and beans
céleri celeriac
cèpe cepe (*mushroom*)
cervelle maître d'Hôtel brains
champignon de Paris champignon (*cultivated mushroom*)
chausson aux pommes apple turnover
chevreuil venison
chocolatine chocolate-filled bun
choucroute sauerkraut with sausages etc
chou de Bruxelles Brussels sprout
civet game stew
clafoutis fruit pudding cooked in the oven
colin mayonnaise hake with mayonnaise
confit d'oie goose preserve
coq au vin chicken in red wine
coquille Saint-Jacques scallop
côte de porc pork chop
cotelette de mouton lamb chop
coulis de framboises raspberry sauce
coulis de langoustines saltwater crayfish sauce
couscous semolina with meat, vegetables and hot spicy broth
crème cream, creamy sauce or dessert
crème anglaise custard
crème renversée dessert in a mould
crêpe aux fruits de mer seafood pancake
crêpes Suzette flambéed orange pancakes
cresson watercress
crevette grise shrimp
crevette rose prawn
croque-monsieur toasted cheese sandwich with ham
crudités selection of salads, chopped raw vegetables
cuisses de grenouille frogs' legs

daube beef stew in red wine
daurade gilthead (*fish*)
diabolo menthe mint cordial with lemonade

MENU READER

échalote shallot
écrevisses à la nage freshwater crayfish in wine and vegetable broth
endive chicory, endive
endives au jambon endives with ham done in oven
entrecôte rib steak
entrée starter, first course
épaule d'agneau farcie stuffed shoulder of lamb
épinards à la creme spinach with cream
escalope panée breaded escalope
escargots à la bourguignonne snails in garlic butter

faisan pheasant
fenouil fennel
financière rich sauce, served with sweetbread and dumplings
flageolet kidney bean
flan custard tart, crème caramel
flétan halibut
foie de veau calves' liver
foie gras fine liver pâté
foies de volaille chicken livers
fondue Swiss dish of cheese melted in white wine
fondue bourguignonne meat fondue
frisée aux lardons curly endive with bacon

galantine cold meat and pâté in aspic
galette round flat biscuit
garni with potatoes and vegetables
gaufre wafer
gelée jelly
gigot d'agneau leg of lamb
grand veneur sauce for game
gratin dauphinois potatoes with grated cheese
grillade grilled meat
groseille rouge red currant

hachis Parmentier shepherd's pie
hareng mariné marinated herring
haricot de mouton mutton stew with beans

MENU READER

homard à l'américaine lobster with tomato and white wine sauce
huître oyster

îles flottantes floating islands
infusion herb tea

jarret de veau shin of veal
julienne soup with chopped vegetables

langue de boeuf ox tongue
lapin aux pruneaux rabbit with prunes
lentille lentil
lièvre hare
limande dab, lemon sole
lotte monkfish
loup flambé au pastis bass flambéed with pastis

macédoine de légumes mixed vegetables
magret de canard duck breast
maquereau au vin blanc mackerel pickled in white wine
merlan au vin blanc whiting in white wine
millefeuille cream slice
morue cod
moules marinières mussels in white wine
mousse au chocolat chocolate mousse
mouton mutton

nature plain
navarin mutton stew with vegetables
navet turnip

oeuf poché poached egg
oeufs à la neige floating islands
oeuf sur le plat fried egg
omelette au fromage cheese omelette
omelette aux champignons mushroom omelette
omelette aux pommes de terre potato omelette
orange givrée orange sorbet served in the scooped-out orange
oseille sorrel

oursin sea urchin

palourde clam
pané breaded
pâté de campagne coarse pâté
pâté de foie de volailles chicken liver pâté
paupiettes de veau rolled up stuffed slice of veal
perdrix aux choux partridge with cabbage
petite friture whitebait
pieds de porc pigs' trotters
pilaf rice dish with meat, pilaf
pintade guinea fowl
plateau de fruits de mer seafood platter
poire belle-Hélène pear in chocolate sauce
poivron pepper
pommes (de terre) sautées sautéed or fried potatoes
pommes vapeur boiled potatoes
potage velouté creamy soup
pot-au-feu beef and vegetable stew
potée meat and vegetable hotpot
poule au pot boiled chicken
poulet à l'estragon chicken in tarragon sauce
poulet basquaise chicken with ham, tomatoes and
  peppers
poulet chasseur chicken with mushrooms and white
  wine
poulet rôti roast chicken
pruneau prune
purée mashed potatoes

quenelle meat or fish dumpling
quiche lorraine quiche with eggs and bacon

raclette Swiss dish of melted cheese
ragoût stew
ratatouille Mediterranean vegetables cooked in olive oil
rillettes potted pork and goose meat
ris de veau veal sweetbread
rognons au madère kidneys in Madeira wine
rôti de porc roast pork
rouget en papillote mullet cooked in foil

MENU READER

saignant rare
salade composée mixed salad
salade niçoise salad with olives, tomatoes and anchovies
salsifis oyster plant, salsify
sanglier wild boar
sauce béarnaise sauce made from egg yolks, lemon juice or vinegar, butter and herbs
sauce hollandaise rich sauce served with fish
sauce Mornay béchamel sauce (*made of cream, butter and flour*) with cheese
saucisson salami-type sausage
saumon fumé smoked salmon
soufflé au fromage cheese soufflé
soupe de légumes vegetable soup
soupe de poissons fish soup
steak au poivre pepper steak
steak frites steak and chips
steak haché beefburger
steak tartare raw minced beef served with a raw egg
sucrette sweetener

tarte tatin baked apple dish
tartine buttered slice of bread
terrine pâté
thé à la menthe mint tea
thé citron lemon tea
tilleul lime tea
tomates farcies stuffed tomatoes
tournedos fillet steak
tripes à la mode de Caen tripe in wine with vegetables and herbs
truite aux amandes trout with almonds
truite meunière fried trout

velouté de volaille cream of chicken soup
vermicelle very fine pasta used in soups
verveine verbena tea
vichyssoise cold vegetable soup

HAVING A DRINK

bar	un bar *bar*
beer	une bière *byair*
coke (R)	un coca *koka*
dry	sec *sek*
fresh orange	un jus d'orange *jew doronj*
gin and tonic	un gin-tonic *jeen-toneek*
ice	la glace *glahss*
lager	une bière blonde *byair blonD*
lemonade	une limonade *leemonahd*
pub	un bistro *beestro*
red	rouge *rooj*
straight	sec *sek*
sweet	doux *doo*
vodka	la vodka *voDka*
whisky	un whisky *weeskee*
white	blanc *blon*
wine	le vin *van*

let's go for a drink
on va boire un pot ?
on va bwahr an po

a beer please
une bière, s'il vous plaît
ewn byair seelvooplay

two beers please
deux bières, s'il vous plaît
duh byair seelvooplay

a glass of red/white wine
un verre de vin rouge/blanc
an vair duh van rooj/blan

with lots of ice
avec beaucoup de glace
avek bokoo duh glahss

25

HAVING A DRINK

no ice thanks
sans glace, s'il vous plaît
son glahss seelvooplay

can I have another one?
remettez-moi ça
ruhmetay-mwa sa

the same again please
la même chose, s'il vous plaît
la mem shoz seelvooplay

what'll you have?
qu'est-ce que vous prenez ?
keskuh voo pruhnay

I'll get this round
c'est ma tournée
say ma toornay

not for me thanks
pas pour moi, merci
pa poor mwa mairsee

he's absolutely smashed
il est complètement rond
eel ay konpletmon ron

bière (blonde)	lager
bière brune	stout
blanc	white wine
brasserie	café-restaurant
café	black coffee
crème	white coffee (*small cup*)
demi	third of a litre of beer
grand crème	white coffee (*large cup*)
kir	blackcurrant liqueur with white wine
pression	draught
rouge	red wine
tarif des consommations	price list

COLLOQUIAL EXPRESSIONS

barmy	dingue *daNg*
bastard	salaud *sahlo*
bird	une nana *nana*
bloke	un mec *mek*
boozer (*pub*)	un bistro *beestro*
nutter	un cinglé *saNglay*
pissed	bourré *booray*
thickie	un imbécile *aNbayseel*
twit	un crétin *kraytaN*

great!
super !
soopair

that's awful!
quelle horreur !
kel orur

shut up!
ferme-la !
fairm-la

ouch!
aïe !
'eye'

yum-yum!
miam!
mee-am

I'm absolutely knackered
je suis complètement crevé
juh swee koNpletmoN kruhvay

I'm fed up
j'en ai marre
joNay mar

COLLOQUIAL EXPRESSIONS

I'm fed up with ...
j'en ai ras le bol de ...
joNay ralbol duh

don't make me laugh!
laissez-moi rire !
lessay-mwa reer

you've got to be joking!
vous plaisantez !
voo playzoNtay!

it's rubbish (*goods etc*)
c'est de la camelotte
say duh la kamlot

it's a rip-off
c'est du vol organisé
say dew vol organeezay

get lost!
tire-toi !
teer-twa

it's a nuisance
c'est vraiment embêtant
say vraymoN oNbetoN

it's absolutely fantastic
c'est vraiment génial
say vraimoN jaynyal

ça alors !	I don't believe it!
ça va	it's OK/I'm OK
c'est ça	that's it
c'est marrant	it's fun(ny)
chauffard !	learn to drive!
copain	chum
dingue	crazy
fous le camp !	get lost!
truc	thing

GETTING AROUND

bike	un vélo *vaylo*
bus	l'autobus *m otobewss*
car	une voiture *vwatewr*
change (*trains*)	changer *shonjay*
garage (*for fuel*)	un garage *garahj*
hitch-hike	faire du stop *fair dew stop*
map	une carte *kart*
moped	une mobylette *mobeelet*
motorbike	une moto *moto*
petrol	l'essence *f essonss*
return (ticket)	un aller retour *alay ruhtoor*
single	un aller simple *alay saNpl*
station	la gare *gar*
taxi	un taxi *taxee*
ticket (*train*)	un billet *beeyay*
(*bus, underground*)	un ticket *teekay*
train	le train *traN*
underground	le métro *maytro*

I'd like to rent a car/ bike/ moped
j'aimerais louer une voiture/ un vélo/ une mobylette
jemray loo-ay ewn vwatewr/ aN vaylo/ ewn mobeelet

how much is it per day?
combien ça coûte par jour ?
koNbyaN sa koot par joor

when do I have to bring the car back?
quand dois-je rapporter la voiture ?
koN dwaj raportay la vwatewr

I'm heading for ...
je vais à ...
juh veza

how do I get to ...?
par où est ...?
par oo ay

GETTING AROUND

REPLIES

tout droit
too drwa
straight on

tournez à gauche/ droite
toornay za gohsh/ drwaht
turn left/ right

c'est ce bâtiment-là
say suh bah-teemoN-la
it's that building there

il faut revenir sur vos pas
eel fo ruhvuhneer sewr vo pa
it's back that way

la première/ deuxième/ troisième à gauche
la pruhmee-air/ duhzee-em/ trwazee-em ah gohsh
first/ second/ third on the left

we're just travelling around
nous visitons la région
noo veezeetoN la rayjee-oN

I'm a stranger here
je ne suis pas d'ici
juh nuh swee pa deessee

is that on the way?
est-ce sur mon chemin ?
ess sewr moN shumaN

can I get off here?
est-ce que je peux descendre ici ?
eskuh juh puh dessoNdr eessee

thanks very much for the lift
merci de m'avoir emmené
mairsee duh mavwahr oNmnay

two returns to . . . please
deux aller retour pour . . ., s'il vous plaît
duh zalay ruhtoor poor . . . seelvooplay

what time is the last train back?
à quelle heure part le dernier train pour rentrer ?
ah kel ur par luh dairnyay traN poor roNtray

we want to leave tomorrow and come back the day after
nous voulons partir demain et revenir après-demain
noo vooloN parteer duhmaN ay ruhvuhneer apray-duhmaN

we're coming back the same day
nous reviendrons dans la journée
noo ruhvyaNdroN doN la joornay

is this the right platform for ...?
c'est bien le quai pour aller à ... ?
say byaN luh kay poor alay ah

is this train going to ...?
c'est bien le train pour ... ?
say byaN luh traN poor

which station is this?
où sommes-nous ?
oo som-noo

which stop is it for ...?
où est-ce que je dois descendre pour aller à ... ?
oo eskuh juh dwa dessoNdr poor alay ah

is there any sort of runabout ticket?
est-ce qu'il y a des billets circulaires ?
eskeel ya day beeyay seerkewlair

can I take my bike on the train?
est-ce que je peux emporter mon vélo ?
eskuh juh puh oNportay moN vaylo

how far is it to the nearest petrol station?
où se trouve la station-service la plus proche ?
oo suh troov la stass-yoN serveess la plew prosh

I need a new tyre
j'ai besoin d'un pneu neuf
jay buhzwaN daN pnuh nuhf

it's overheating
le moteur chauffe
luh motur shof

31

GETTING AROUND

there's something wrong with the brakes
les freins ne marchent pas bien
lay fran nuh marsh pa byan

arrivée	arrival(s)
autoroute	motorway
carnet	book of underground tickets
carte orange	season ticket (*Paris*)
cédez le passage	give way
départ	departure(s)
déviation	diversion
distributeur de billets	ticket machine
fin de ...	end of ...
gare routière	bus station
grandes lignes	main lines
guichet	ticket office
jours impairs	odd dates of the month (*parking allowed*)
jours pairs	even dates of the month (*parking allowed*)
M, métro	underground
ne pas se pencher par la fenêtre	do not lean out of the window
péage	toll
pour ouvrir appuyer	push to open
priorité à droite	vehicles coming from the right have priority
quai	platform
RER	fast suburban train in Paris
sans plomb	lead-free
stationnement gênant	no parking please
stationnement interdit	no parking
TGV	high-speed train
travaux	roadworks
l'usage des WC est interdit pendant l'arrêt du train en gare	do not use the toilet while the train is in a station
zone bleue	restricted parking area

32

carrier bag	un sac *sak*
cashdesk	la caisse *kess*
cheap	bon marché *bon marshay*
cheque	un chèque *shek*
department	le rayon *rayon*
expensive	cher *shair*
pay	payer *payay*
receipt	un reçu *ruhsew*
shop	un magasin *magazan*
shop assistant	le vendeur *vondur*
	la vendeuse *vondurz*
supermarket	le supermarché *sewpairmarshay*
till	la caisse *kess*

I'd like ...
j'aimerais ...
jemray

have you got ...?
avez-vous ... ?
avay-voo

how much is this?
c'est combien ?
say konbyan

can I just have a look around?
je peux regarder ?
juh puh ruhgarday

the one in the window
l'article en vitrine
larteekl on veetreen

do you take credit cards ?
vous acceptez les cartes de crédit ?
voo zakseptay lay kart duh kraydee

SHOPPING

could I have a receipt please?
je peux avoir un reçu ?
juh puh avwahr an ruhsew

I'd like to try it on
j'aimerais l'essayer
jemray lessayay

I'll come back
je reviendrai
juh ruh-vyandray

it's too big/ small
c'est trop grand/ petit
say tro gron/ ptee

it's not what I'm looking for
ce n'est pas ce qu'il me faut
suh nay pa sukeel muh fo

I'll take it
j'aimerais l'acheter
jemray lashtay

can you gift-wrap it?
vous pouvez me faire un emballage-cadeau ?
voo poovay muh fair an onbalahj-kado

alimentation	food
caisse	till
conserver au frais	keep in a cool place
consommer avant le . . .	best before . . .
date limite de vente	sell-by date
fermé	closed
horaire d'ouverture	opening times
payez à la caisse	pay at the desk
prenez un caddy	take a trolley
prêt-à-porter	clothes
rabais	reduction
soldes	sale
tabac	tobacconist and newsagent

34

FRANCE AND THINGS FRENCH

Some names which are different in French:

Brittany	la Bretagne *bruh-tan*
Corsica	la Corse *korss*
Eiffel Tower	la Tour Eiffel *toor ayfel*
French Riviera	la Côte d'Azur *koht dazewr*
Paris	Paris *paree*
South of France	le Midi *meedee*
arrondissement	administrative district of Paris
bal du 14 juillet	dance on French national holiday (*14th July — katorz jwee-ay*)
bateau-mouche	pleasure boat on the Seine
château	castle
circuit touristique	touristic route
cuisses de grenouille	frogs' legs (*literally: thighs*)
dégustation gratuite	free wine-tasting
département	administrative district of France
fête nationale	July 14th, national holiday
l'hexagone	France (*colloquial term*)
hôtel de ville	town hall
le Midi	South of France
le Quartier Latin	the Latin Quarter in Paris (atmospheric student/ artist area, lots of cafés etc)
le quinze août	August 15th, a national holiday
la rive droite	right bank or side (of Seine in Paris)
la rive gauche	left bank or side (of Seine in Paris)
roman	Romanesque
la route du vin	route taking in vineyards
le seizième	the 16th 'arrondissement', up-market area of Paris
le syndicat d'initiative	tourist information office
vieille ville	old town

35

bank	une banque *boNk*
bill	l'addition *f adeessyoN*
bureau de change	un bureau de change *bewro duh shoNj*
cash dispenser	un distributeur de billets *deestreebewtur duh beeyay*
change (*small*)	la monnaie *monay*
cheque	un chèque *shek*
credit card	une carte de crédit *kart duh kraydee*
Eurocheque	un eurochèque *uhroshek*
exchange rate	le taux de change *to duh shoNj*
expensive	cher *shair*
French francs	les francs français *froN froNsay*
pounds (sterling)	les livres sterling *leevr stairleen*
price	le prix *pree*
receipt	un reçu *ruhsew*
traveller's cheque	un chèque de voyage *shek duh vwoyahj*

how much is it?
combien ça coûte ?
koNbyaN sa koot

I'd like to change this into . . .
j'aimerais changer ceci en . . .
jemray shoNjay suh-see oN

can you give me something smaller?
pourriez-vous me donner de la monnaie ?
poor-yay voo muh donay duh la monay

can I use this credit card?
est-ce que vous acceptez cette carte de crédit ?
eskuh voo zakseptay set kart duh kraydee

can we have the bill please?
l'addition, s'il vous plaît
ladeessyoN seelvooplay

MONEY

please keep the change
gardez la monnaie
garday la monay

does that include service?
est-ce que le service est compris ?
eskuh luh sairveess ay konpree

what are your rates?
quels sont vos taux ?
kel son vo to

I think the figures are wrong
je crois qu'il y a une erreur
juh krwa keel ya ewn airur

I'm completely skint
je n'ai pas un rond
juh nay pa zan ron

The unit is the 'franc' *fron*, which is divided into 100
'centimes' *sonteem*. A colloquial word for money is 'le
fric' *freek*.

achat	purchase, buying rate
banque	bank
caisse d'épargne	savings bank
carte de crédit	credit card
change	change
livre sterling	pound sterling
taux de change	exchange rate
TVA	VAT
vente	sale, selling rate

band (*pop*)	le groupe *groop*
cinema	le cinéma *seenayma*
concert	le concert *konsair*
disco	une discothèque *deeskotayk*
film	un film *feelm*
go out	sortir *sorteer*
music	la musique *mewzeek*
night out	une soirée *swahray*
play (*theatre*)	une pièce *pee-ess*
seat	une place *plass*
show	un spectacle *spektakl*
singer	un chanteur *shontur*
	une chanteuse *shonturz*
theatre	le théâtre *tay-ahtr*
ticket	un billet *beeyay*

are you doing anything tonight?
qu'est-ce que tu fais ce soir ?
keskuh tew fay suh swahr

do you want to come out with me tonight?
veux-tu sortir avec moi ce soir ?
vuh-tew sorteer avek mwa suh swahr

what's on?
qu'est-ce qu'il y a comme spectacles ?
keskeel ya kom spektakl

have you got a programme of what's on in town?
avez-vous un programme des spectacles en ville ?
avay-voo an program day spektakl on veel

which is the best disco round here?
quelle est la meilleure discothèque du coin ?
kel ay la mayur deeskotek dew kwan

let's go to the cinema/ theatre
allons au cinéma/ théâtre
alon zo seenayma/ tay-ahtr

ENTERTAINMENT

I've seen it
je l'ai déjà vu
juh lay dayja vew

I'll meet you at 9 o'clock at the station
rendez-vous à la gare à 9 heures
roɴday-voo ah la gar ah nurf ur

can I have two tickets for tonight's performance?
j'aimerais deux places pour ce soir
jemray duh plass poor suh swahr

do you want to dance?
tu veux danser avec moi ?
tew vuh doɴsay avek mwa

do you want to dance again?
veux-tu danser encore une fois ?
vuh-tew doɴsay oɴkor ewn fwa

thanks but I'm with my boyfriend
merci, mais je suis avec mon copain
mairsee may juh swee zavek moɴ kopaɴ

let's go out for some fresh air
allons prendre l'air
aloɴ proɴdr lair

will you let me back in again later?
vous me laisserez rentrer quand je reviendrai ?
voo muh lessray roɴtray koɴ juh ruh-vyaɴdray

I'm meeting someone inside
j'ai rendez-vous avec quelqu'un à l'intérieur
jay roɴday-voo avek kelkaɴ ah laɴtairyur

annulé	cancelled
entracte	interval
guichet	box office
prix des places	ticket prices
prochaine séance à 20 h	next showing at 8 pm
relâche	closed
sous-titré	with subtitles
VO	in the original language

THE BEACH

beach	la plage *plahj*
beach umbrella	un parasol *parasol*
bikini	un bikini *beekeenee*
dive	plonger *plonjay*
sand	le sable *sahbl*
sea	la mer *mair*
sunbathe	se bronzer *suh bronzay*
suntan lotion	le lait solaire *lay solair*
suntan oil	l'huile *f* *weel*
swim	nager *na-jay*
swimming costume	un costume de bain *kostewm duh ban*
tan (*verb*)	bronzer *bronzay*
towel	une serviette éponge *sairvee-et ayponj*
wave	la vague *vahg*

let's go down to the beach
allons à la plage
alon za la plahj

what's the water like?
elle est bonne ?
el ay bon

it's freezing
elle est glacée
el ay glasay

it's beautiful
elle est bonne
el ay bon

are you coming for a swim?
vous venez nager ?
voo vuh-nay na-jay

I can't swim
je ne sais pas nager
juh nuh say pa na-jay

he swims like a fish
il nage comme un poisson
eel nahj kom an pwasson

will you keep an eye on my things for me?
pouvez-vous garder mes affaires ?
poovay-voo garday may zafair

is it deep here?
l'eau est profonde ?
lo ay profond

could you rub suntan oil on my back?
tu peux me passer de l'huile sur le dos ?
tew puh muh pa-say duh lweel sewr luh do

I love sun bathing
j'adore me faire bronzer
jador muh fair bronzay

I'm all sunburnt
j'ai pris un gros coup de soleil
jay pree zan gro koodsolay

you're all wet!
tu es tout mouillé !
tew ay too moo-yay

let's go up to the cafe
on va au café ?
on va o kafay

à louer	for hire
baignade dangereuse	it is dangerous to swim here
baignade interdite	no swimming
douches	showers
glaces	ice-cream
location de . . .	. . . for hire
surveillant de plage	lifeguard

accident	un accident *akseedon*
ambulance	une ambulance *onbewlonss*
broken	cassé *kassay*
doctor	un médecin *maydsan*
emergency	une urgence *ewrjonss*
fire	un incendie *ansondee*
fire brigade	les pompiers *mpl ponpyay*
ill	malade *malad*
injured	blessé *blessay*
late	en retard *on ruhtar*
out of order	en dérangement *on dayronjmon*
police	la police *poleess*

can you help me? I'm lost
pouvez-vous m'aider ? je me suis perdu
poovay-voo mayday — juh muh swee pairdew

I've lost my passport
j'ai perdu mon passeport
jay perdew mon paspor

I've locked myself out of my room
je me suis enfermé dehors
juh muh swee zonfairmay duh-or

my luggage hasn't arrived
mes bagages ne sont pas arrivés
may bagahj nuh son pa zareevay

I can't get it open
je n'arrive pas à l'ouvrir
juh nareev pa za loovreer

it's jammed
c'est bloqué
say blokay

I don't have enough money
je n'ai pas assez d'argent
juh nay pa zassay darjon

I've broken down
je suis tombé en panne
juh swee tonbay on pan

can I use your telephone please, this is an emergency
est-ce que je peux me servir de votre téléphone ? il s'agit
d'une urgence
*eskuh juh puh muh sairveer duh votr taylayfon — eel sajee
dewn ewrjonss*

help!
au secours !
o skoor

it doesn't work
ça ne marche pas
sa nuh marsh pa

the lights aren't working in my room
la lumière ne marche pas dans ma chambre
la lewmyair nuh marsh pa don ma shonbr

the lift is stuck
l'ascenseur est en panne
lassonsur ay ton pan

I can't understand a single word
je ne comprends rien
juh nuh konpron ryan

can you get an interpreter?
pouvez-vous trouver quelqu'un pour traduire ?
poovay-voo troovay kelkan poor tradweer

the toilet won't flush
la chasse d'eau ne marche pas
la shass doh nuh marsh pa

there's no plug in the bath
il n'y a pas de bonde pour la baignoire
eel nya pa duh bond poor la benwahr

PROBLEMS

there's no hot water
il n'y a pas d'eau chaude
eel nya pa do shohd

there's no toilet paper left
il n'y a plus de papier hygiénique
eel nya plew duh papee-ay eejee-ayneek

I'm afraid I've accidentally broken the . . .
je suis désolé, j'ai cassé le/ la . . .
juh swee dayzolay jay kassay luh/ la

this man has been following me
cet homme me suit depuis un moment
set om muh swee duh-pwee zaɴ momoɴ

I've been mugged
j'ai été agressé
jay aytay agressay

my handbag has been stolen
on m'a volé mon sac à main
oɴ ma volay moɴ sakamaɴ

attention	caution
attention, chien méchant	beware of the dog
défense de . . .	no . . .
en panne	out of order
hors service	out of order
interdit	prohibited
objets trouvés	lost property office
police secours	emergency police (*999*)
sortie de secours	emergency exit
SOS Femmes	Women's Aid Centre, Rape Crisis Centre etc

HEALTH

bandage	le pansement *ponsmon*
blood	le sang *son*
broken	cassé *kassay*
burn	la brûlure *brewlewr*
chemist's	la pharmacie *farmasee*
contraception	la contraception *kontrassepsyon*
dentist	un dentiste *donteest*
disabled	handicapé *ondeekapay*
disease	une maladie *maladee*
doctor	un médecin *maydsan*
health	la santé *sontay*
hospital	un hôpital *opeetal*
ill	malade *malad*
nurse	une infirmière *anfeermyair*
wound	une blessure *blessewr*

I don't feel well
je ne me sens pas bien
juh nuh muh son pa byan

it's getting worse
ça empire
sa onpeer

I feel better
je me sens mieux
juh muh son m-yuh

I feel sick
j'ai mal au cœur
jay mal o kur

I've got a pain here
j'ai mal ici
jay mal eessee

it hurts
ça fait mal
sa fay mal

HEALTH

he's got a high temperature
il a beaucoup de fièvre
eel ah bokoo duh fee-evr

could you call a doctor?
pouvez-vous appeler un médecin ?
poovay-voo aplay aN maydsaN

is it serious?
c'est grave ?
say grahv

will he need an operation?
il faudra l'opérer ?
eel fo-dra lopairay

I'm diabetic
je suis diabétique
juh swee dee-abeteek

keep her warm
il faut qu'elle reste au chaud
eel fo kel rest o sho

have you got anything for . . .?
avez-vous quelque chose contre . . . ?
avay-voo kelkuh-shoz koNtr

agiter avant l'emploi	shake before use
analgésique	painkiller
à prendre à jeun	to be taken on an empty stomac
à prendre avant/après les repas	to be taken before/after meals
cabinet médical	doctor's surgery
calmant	tranquilizer
diluer	dissolve
ne pas avaler	do not swallow
SAMU	emergency medical service
somnifère	sleeping pill
un comprimé par jour	one tablet a day
vendu uniquement sur ordonnance	sold on prescription only

I want to learn to sailboard
j'aimerais apprendre à faire de la planche à voile
jemray zaprondr ah fair duh la plonsh ah vwal

can we hire a sailing boat?
est-ce que nous pouvons louer un bateau à voile ?
eskuh noo poovon loo-ay an bato ah vwal

how much is half an hour's waterskiing?
combien coûte une demi-heure de ski nautique ?
konbyan koot ewn duhmee-uhr duh ski notik

can we use the tennis court?
est-ce que nous pouvons utiliser le court de tennis ?
eskuh noo poovon uteeleezay luh koor duh tennis

see you at the top of the skilift
rendez-vous à l'arrivée du télésiège
ronday-voo ah lareevay dew telesee-ej

how much is a skipass?
combien coûte un forfait-skieurs ?
konbyan koot an forfay-skee-ur

I'd like to go and watch a football match
j'aimerais aller à un match de football
jemray alay ah an match duh footbal

is it possible to do any horse-riding here?
est-ce qu'on peut faire de l'équitation ici ?
eskon puh fair duh lekeetasyon eesee

we're going to do some hill-walking
nous allons faire des randonnées
noo zallon fair day rondonay

this is the first time I've ever tried it
c'est la première fois que j'en fais
say la pruhmyair fwa kuh jon fay

47

THE POST OFFICE

letter	la lettre *letr*
poste restante	la poste restante *post restoNt*
post office	la poste *posst*
recorded delivery	recommandé *ruh-komoNday*
send	envoyer *oNvwoy-yay*
stamp	un timbre *taNbr*

how much is a letter to Ireland?
quel est le tarif pour envoyer une lettre en Irlande ?
kel ay luh tareef poor oNvwoy-yay ewn letr oN eerloNd

I'd like four 3 franc stamps
j'aimerais quatre timbres à 3 francs
jemray katr taNbr ah trwa froN

I'd like six stamps for postcards to England
j'aimerais six timbres pour des cartes postales à
destination de l'Angleterre
*jemray see taNbr poor day kart postal ah desteenass-yoN duh
loNgluh-tair*

is there any mail for me?
y a-t-il du courrier pour moi ?
ee yateel dew kooree-ay poor mwa

I'm expecting a parcel from ...
j'attends un colis de ...
jatoN zaN kolee duh

affranchissements	letters and postcards
code postal	post code
destinataire	addressee
expéditeur	sender
prochaine levée	next collection
PTT	post office and telephones
timbres	stamps

directory enquiries	les renseignements *mpl* *ronsenyuh-mon*
engaged	occupé *okewpay*
extension	le poste *posst*
number	le numéro *newmairo*
operator	l'opératrice *f opayratreess*
phone (*verb*)	téléphoner *taylayfonay*
phone box	une cabine téléphonique *kabeen taylayfoneek*
phonecard	la télécarte
telephone	le téléphone *taylayfon*
telephone directory	le bottin *botan*

is there a phone round here?
y a-t-il un téléphone par ici ?
yateel an taylayfon par eessee

can I use your phone?
est-ce que je peux me servir de votre téléphone ?
eskuh juh puh muh sairveer duh votr taylayfon

I'd like to make a phone call to Britain
j'aimerais téléphoner en Grande-Bretagne
jemray taylayfonay on grond bruhtan

I want to reverse the charges
je veux téléphoner en PCV
juh vuh taylayfonay on pay-say-vay

could I speak to Patricia?
j'aimerais parler à Patricia
jemray parlay ah Patricia

hello, this is Simon speaking
allô, c'est Simon
alo say Simon

TELEPHONING

can I leave a message?
est-ce que je peux laisser un message ?
eskuh juh puh lessay AN messahj

do you speak English?
vous parlez l'anglais ?
voo parlay longlay

could you say that again very very slowly?
pourriez-vous répéter cela très très lentement ?
poor-yay voo raypaytay suhla tray tray lontmon

could you tell him Jim called?
pouvez-vous lui dire que Jim a appelé ?
poovay-voo lwee deer kuh Jim ah aplay

could you ask her to ring me back?
pouvez-vous lui demander de me rappeler ?
poovay-voo lwee duhmonday duh muh raplay

I'll call back later
je rappellerai
juh rapelray

776-3211
sept-cent soixante-seize trente-deux onze
set son swahsont-sez tront-duh onz

just a minute please
un instant, s'il vous plaît
AN ANSTON seelvooplay

he's not in
il est sorti
eel ay sortee

sorry, I've got the wrong number
excusez-moi, je me suis trompé de numéro
eks-kewzay-mwa, juh muh swee tronpay duh newmairo

it's a terrible line
je vous entends très mal
juh voo zonton tray mal

> **REPLIES**   ne quittez pas
> *nuh keetay pa*
> hang on

50

TELEPHONING

c'est de la part de qui ?
say duh la par duh kee
who shall I say is calling?

qui est à l'appareil ?
kee ayta laparay
who's calling?

bottin	phone book
cette cabine peut être appelée à ce numéro:. . .	incoming calls can be made to the following number: . . .
composez le . . .	dial . . .
décrochez	lift receiver
fermez le volet svp	please close the flap
introduire carte ou faire no. d'urgence	insert card or dial emergency number
numérotez	dial
patientez svp	please wait
pompiers	fire brigade
retirez votre carte	remove your card
Royaume-Uni	UK
télécarte	phonecard
téléphone interurbain	long-distance phone
tonalité	(ringing) tone

THE ALPHABET

how do you spell it?
ça s'écrit comment ?
sa saykree komon

I'll spell it
ça s'écrit . . .
sa saykree

a *ah*	**g** *jay*	**m** *em*	**s** *ess*	**x** *eeks*
b *bay*	**h** *ash*	**n** *en*	**t** *tay*	**y** *ee-grek*
c *say*	**i** *ee*	**o** *o*	**u** *oo*	**z** *zed*
d *day*	**j** *jee*	**p** *pay*	**v** *vay*	
e *uh*	**k** *ka*	**q** *koo*	**w** *doobluh-*	
f *ef*	**l** *el*	**r** *air*	*vay*	

NUMBERS, THE DATE AND THE TIME

0	zéro *zayro*
1	un *aN*
2	deux *duh*
3	trois *trwa*
4	quatre *katr*
5	cinq *saNk*
6	six *seess*
7	sept *set*
8	huit *weet*
9	neuf *nuhf*
10	dix *deess*
11	onze *oNz*
12	douze *dooz*
13	treize *trez*
14	quartorze *katorz*
15	quinze *kaNz*
16	seize *sez*
17	dix-sept *deeset*
18	dix-huit *deez-weet*
19	dix-neuf *deez-nuhf*
20	vingt *vaN*
21	vingt et un *vaNtay-aN*
22	vingt-deux *vaN-duh*
30	trente *troNt*
35	trente-cinq *troNt-saNk*
40	quarante *karoNt*
50	cinquante *saNkoNt*
60	soixante *swassoNt*
70	soixante-dix *swassoNt-deess*
80	quatre-vingts *katr-vaN*
90	quatre-vingt-dix *katr-vaN-deess*
91	quatre-vingt-onze *katr-vaN-oNz*
100	cent *soN*

NUMBERS, THE DATE, THE TIME

101	cent un	*son an*
200	deux cents	*duh son*
202	deux cent deux	*duh son duh*
1,000	mille	*meel*
2,000	deux mille	*duh meel*
1,000,000	un million	*an meel-yon*
1st	premier	*pruhmyay*
2nd	deuxième	*duhzee-em*
3rd	troisième	*trwazee-em*
4th	quatrième	*katree-em*
5th	cinquième	*sankee-em*
6th	sixième	*seezee-em*
7th	septième	*setee-em*
8th	huitième	*weetee-em*
9th	neuvième	*nuhvee-em*
10th	dixième	*deezee-em*

what's the date?
quel jour sommes-nous ?
kel joor som-noo

it's the first of June
nous sommes le premier juin
noo som luh pruhmyay jwan

it's the tenth/ twelfth of May 1994
nous sommes le 10/ 12 mai mille neuf cent quatre-
vingt-quatorze
noo som luh deess/ dooz may meel-nuhf-son-katr-van-kutorz

what time is it?
quelle heure est-il ?
kel ur ay-teel

it's midday/ midnight
il est midi/ minuit
eel ay meedee/ meenwee

it's one/ three o'clock
il est une heure/ trois heures
eel ay tewn ur/ trwa zur

NUMBERS, THE DATE, THE TIME

it's twenty past three/ twenty to three
il est trois heures vingt/ moins vingt
eel ay trwa zur van/ mwan van

it's half past eight
il est huit heures et demie
eel ay wee tur ay duhmee

it's a quarter past/ a quarter to five
il est cinq heures et quart/ moins le quart
eel ay sank ur ay kar/ mwan luh kar

at two/ five p.m.
à quatorze/ dix-sept heures
ah katorz/ dee-set ur

A

a un, f une (see grammar)
about (approx) environ
above au-dessus de
abroad à l'étranger
accelerator l'accélérateur m
accent l'accent m
accept accepter
accident l'accident m
accommodation le logement
accompany accompagner
ache la douleur
adaptor (for voltage) l'adaptateur m; (plug) la prise multiple
address l'adresse f
address book le carnet d'adresses
adult l'adulte m
advance: in advance d'avance
advise conseiller
aeroplane l'avion m
afraid: I'm afraid (of) j'ai peur (de)
after après
afternoon l'après-midi m
aftershave l'after-shave m
afterwards ensuite
again de nouveau
against contre
age l'âge m
agency l'agence f
agent le représentant; (for cars) le concessionnaire
aggressive agressif

ago: three days ago il y a trois jours
agree: I agree je suis d'accord
AIDS le SIDA
air l'air m
air-conditioned climatisé
air-conditioning la climatisation
air hostess l'hôtesse de l'air f
airline la compagnie aérienne
airmail: by airmail par avion
airport l'aéroport m
alarm l'alarme f
alarm clock le réveil
alcohol l'alcool m
alive vivant
all: all men/ women tous les hommes/ toutes les femmes; **all the milk/ beer** tout le lait/ toute la bière; **all day** toute la journée
allergic to allergique à
all-inclusive tout compris
allow permettre
allowed permis
all right: that's all right d'accord
almost presque
alone seul
already déjà
also aussi
alternator l'alternateur m
although bien que
altogether en tout
always toujours
a.m.: at 5 a.m. à 5 heures du matin
ambulance l'ambulance f

America l'Amérique *f*
American américain
among parmi
amp: 15-amp de 15 ampères
ancestor l'ancêtre *m*
anchor l'ancre *f*
ancient ancien
and et
angina l'angine de poitrine *f*
angry fâché
animal l'animal *m*
ankle la cheville
anniversary (*wedding*)
l'anniversaire de mariage *m*
annoying ennuyeux
anorak l'anorak *m*
another un/une autre;
another beer encore une
bière
answer la réponse
answer (*verb*) répondre
ant la fourmi
antibiotic l'antibiotique *m*
antifreeze l'antigel *m*
antihistamine
l'antihistaminique *m*
antique: it's an antique c'est
un objet d'époque
antique shop l'antiquaire *m*
antiseptic le désinfectant
**any: have you got any butter/
bananas?** avez-vous du
beurre/ des bananes ?; **I
don't have any** je n'en ai
pas
anyway quand-même
apartment l'appartement *m*
aperitif l'apéritif *m*
apologize s'excuser
appalling épouvantable
appendicitis l'appendicite *f*
appetite l'appétit *m*
apple la pomme

apple pie la tarte aux
pommes
appointment le rendez-vous
apricot l'abricot *m*
April avril
archaeology l'archéologie *f*
area la région
arm le bras
arrest arrêter
arrival l'arrivée *f*
arrive arriver
art l'art *m*
art gallery le musée d'art
artificial artificiel
artist l'artiste *m*
as (*since*) comme; **as beautiful
as** aussi beau que
ashamed honteux
ashtray le cendrier
ask demander
asleep endormi
asparagus les asperges *fpl*
aspirin l'aspirine *f*
asthma l'asthme *m*
astonishing étonnant
at: at the station à la gare; **at
Betty's** chez Betty; **at 3
o'clock** à 3 heures
Atlantic l'Atlantique *m*
attractive séduisant
aubergine l'aubergine *f*
audience le public
August août
aunt la tante
Australia l'Australie *f*
Australian australien
Austria l'Autriche *f*
automatic automatique
autumn l'automne *m*
awake réveillé
awful affreux
axe la hache
axle l'essieu *m*

B

baby le bébé
baby-sitter le/ la baby-sitter
bachelor le célibataire
back l'arrière *m*; *(of body)* le dos; **the back wheel/ seat** la roue/ le siège arrière
backpack le sac à dos
bacon le lard
bad mauvais
badly mal
bag le sac; *(suitcase)* la valise
bake cuire
baker's la boulangerie
balcony le balcon
bald chauve
ball *(large)* le ballon; *(small)* la balle
banana la banane
bandage le pansement
bank la banque
bar le bar
barbecue le barbecue
barber le coiffeur
barmaid la serveuse
barman le barman
basement le sous-sol
basket le panier
bath le bain
bathing cap le bonnet de bain
bathroom la salle de bain
bath salts les sels de bain *mpl*
bathtub la baignoire
battery la pile; *(for car)* la batterie
be être *(see grammar)*
beach la plage
beans les haricots *mpl*; **green beans** les haricots verts *mpl*
beard la barbe

beautiful beau, *f* belle
because parce que
become devenir
bed le lit; **single/ double bed** lit pour une personne/ deux personnes; **go to bed** aller se coucher
bed linen les draps de lit *mpl*
bedroom la chambre à coucher
bee l'abeille *f*
beef le bœuf
beer la bière
before avant
begin commencer
beginner le débutant
beginning le début
behind derrière
beige beige
Belgian belge
Belgium la Belgique
believe croire
bell la cloche; *(for door)* la sonnette
belong appartenir
below sous
belt la ceinture
bend le virage
best: the best le/ la meilleur
better mieux
between entre
bicycle le vélo
big grand
bikini le bikini
bill la note; *(in restaurant)* l'addition *f*
binding *(ski)* la fixation
bird l'oiseau *m*
biro *(R)* le stylo à bille
birthday l'anniversaire *m*; **happy birthday!** bon anniversaire !
biscuit le petit gâteau

bit: a little bit un peu
bite la morsure; (*insect*) la piqûre
bitter amer
black noir
black and white noir et blanc
blackberry la mûre
bladder la vessie
blanket la couverture
bleach l'eau de Javel *f*
bleed saigner
bless: bless you! santé !
blind aveugle
blister l'ampoule *f*
blocked bouché
blond blond
blood le sang
blood group le groupe sanguin
blouse le chemisier
blow-dry le brushing
blue bleu
boarding pass la carte d'embarquement
boat le bateau
body le corps
boil bouillir
bolt le verrou
bolt (*verb*) verrouiller
bomb la bombe
bone l'os *m*; (*in fish*) l'arête *f*
bonnet (*car*) le capot
book le livre
book (*verb*) réserver
bookshop la librairie
boot (*shoe*) la botte; (*car*) le coffre
border la frontière
boring ennuyeux
born: I was born in 1963 je suis né en 1963
borrow emprunter
boss le patron

both: both of them tous les deux
bottle la bouteille
bottle-opener l'ouvre-bouteille *m*
bottom le fond; (*of body*) le derrière; **at the bottom of** au fond de
bowl le bol
box la boîte
box office le guichet
boy le garçon
boyfriend le petit ami
bra le soutien-gorge
bracelet le bracelet
brake le frein
brake (*verb*) freiner
brandy le cognac
brave courageux
bread le pain; **white/ wholemeal bread** le pain blanc/ complet
break casser
break down tomber en panne
breakdown (*car*) la panne; (*nervous*) la dépression
breakfast le petit déjeuner
breast le sein
breastfeed allaiter
breathe respirer
brick la brique
bridge (*over river*) le pont
briefcase la serviette
bring apporter
Britain la Grande-Bretagne
British britannique
brochure le prospectus
broke: I'm broke je suis fauché
broken cassé
brooch la broche
broom le balai

brother le frère
brother-in-law le beau-frère
brown marron
bruise le bleu
brush la brosse
Brussels sprouts les choux de Bruxelles *mpl*
bucket le seau
building le bâtiment
bulb (*light*) l'ampoule *f*
bull le taureau
bumper le pare-chocs
bunk beds les lits superposés *mpl*
buoy la bouée
burn la brûlure
burn (*verb*) brûler
bus l'autobus *m*
business les affaires *fpl*
business trip le voyage d'affaires
bus station la gare routière
bus stop l'arrêt d'autobus *m*
busy occupé
but mais
butcher's la boucherie
butter le beurre
butterfly le papillon
button le bouton
buy acheter
by par; **by car** en voiture

cabbage le chou
cabin (*ship*) la cabine
cable car le téléférique
café le café
cagoule le K-way
cake le gâteau
cake shop la pâtisserie

calculator la calculette
calendar le calendrier
call appeler
calm down se calmer
Calor gas (*R*) le butagaz
camera (*still*) l'appareil-photo *m*; (*movie*) la caméra
campbed le lit de camp
camping le camping
campsite le camping
can la boîte
can: I/ she can je peux/ elle peut; **can you ...?** pouvez-vous ... ?
Canada le Canada
Canadian canadien
canal le canal
cancel annuler
candle la bougie
canoe le canoë
cap la casquette
captain le capitaine
car la voiture
caravan la caravane
caravan site le terrain pour caravanes
carburettor le carburateur
card la carte; (*business*) la carte de visite
cardboard le carton
cardigan le gilet
car driver l'automobiliste *m*
care: take care of s'occuper de
careful prudent; **be careful!** faites attention !
car park le parking
carpet le tapis; (*fitted*) la moquette
car rental la location de voitures
carriage le wagon
carrot la carotte

carry porter
carry-cot le porte-bébé
cash: pay cash payer comptant
cash desk la caisse
cash dispenser le distribanque
cassette la cassette
cassette player le lecteur de cassettes
castle le château
cat le chat
catch attraper
cathedral la cathédrale
Catholic catholique
cauliflower le chou-fleur
cause la cause
cave la grotte
ceiling le plafond
cemetery le cimetière
centigrade centigrade
central heating le chauffage central
centre le centre
century le siècle
certificate le certificat
chain la chaîne
chair la chaise
chairlift le télésiège
chambermaid la femme de chambre
chance: by chance par hasard
change (small) la monnaie
change (verb) changer; (clothes) se changer; change trains changer de train
changeable (weather) variable
Channel la Manche
charter flight le charter
cheap bon marché
check (verb) vérifier
check-in l'enregistrement des bagages m

cheers! à la vôtre !
cheese le fromage
chemist's la pharmacie
cheque le chèque
cheque book le chéquier
cheque card la carte d'identité bancaire
cherry la cerise
chest la poitrine
chestnut le marron
chewing gum le chewing-gum
chicken la poule; (meat) le poulet
child, pl children l'enfant m
children's portion la portion pour enfants
chin le menton
chips les frites fpl
chocolate le chocolat; milk chocolate le chocolat au lait; plain chocolate le chocolat à croquer; hot chocolate le chocolat chaud
choke (on car) le starter
choose choisir
chop (meat) la côtelette
Christian name le prénom
Christmas Noël
church l'église f
cider le cidre
cigar le cigare
cigarette la cigarette
cinema le cinéma
city la ville
city centre le centre-ville
claret le bordeaux rouge
class la classe; first class la première; second class la seconde
classical music la musique classique
clean (adjective) propre

clean (*verb*) nettoyer
cleansing cream la crème démaquillante
clear (*obvious*) clair
clever intelligent
cliff la falaise
climate le climat
cloakroom (*coats*) le vestiaire
clock l'horloge *f*
close (*verb*) fermer
closed fermé
clothes les vêtements *mpl*
clothes peg la pince à linge
cloud le nuage
cloudy nuageux
club le club
clutch l'embrayage *m*
coach le car
coast la côte
coat le manteau
coathanger le cintre
cockroach le cafard
cocktail le cocktail
cocoa le cacao
coffee le café; **white coffee** le crème
cold froid; **it is cold** il fait froid
cold (*illness*) le rhume; **I've got a cold** je suis enrhumé
cold cream la crème de beauté
collar le col
collection la collection
colour la couleur
colour film la pellicule couleurs
comb le peigne
come venir; **come back** revenir; **come in!** entrez !
comfortable confortable
compact disc le disque compact

company la société
compartment le compartiment
compass la boussole
complain se plaindre
complicated compliqué
compliment le compliment
computer l'ordinateur *m*
concert le concert
conditioner le baume après-shampoing
condom le préservatif
conductor (*bus*) le receveur
confirm confirmer
congratulations! félicitations !
connection la correspondance
constipated constipé
consulate le consulat
contact (*verb*) contacter
contact lenses les lentilles de contact *fpl*
contraceptive le contraceptif
cook le cuisinier
cook (*verb*) cuire
cooker la cuisinière
cooking utensils les ustensiles de cuisine *mpl*
cool frais, *f* fraîche
corkscrew le tire-bouchon
corner le coin
correct correct
corridor le corridor
cosmetics les produits de beauté *mpl*
cost coûter
cot le lit d'enfant
cotton le coton
cotton wool le coton hydrophile
couchette la couchette
cough la toux

cough (*verb*) tousser
country le pays
countryside la campagne
course: of course bien sûr
cousin le cousin, la cousine
cow la vache
crab le crabe
crafts l'artisanat *m*
cramp la crampe
crankshaft le vilebrequin
crash la collision
crayfish la langouste; (*small*) la langoustine
cream la crème
cream puff le chou à la crème
credit card la carte de crédit
crew l'équipage *m*
crisps les chips *fpl*
crockery la vaisselle
cross (*verb*) traverser
crowd la foule
crowded bondé
cruise la croisière
crutches les béquilles *fpl*
cry pleurer
cucumber le concombre
cup la tasse
cupboard l'armoire *f*
curry le curry
curtain le rideau
custom la coutume
customs la douane
cut (*verb*) couper
cutlery les couverts *mpl*
cycling le cyclisme
cyclist le cycliste
cylinder head gasket le joint de culasse

D

dad le papa
damage (*verb*) endommager
damp humide
dance (*verb*) danser
danger le danger
dangerous dangereux
dare oser
dark sombre
dashboard le tableau de bord
date (*time*) la date
daughter la fille
daughter-in-law la belle-fille
day le jour; the day before yesterday avant-hier; the day after tomorrow après-demain
dead mort
deaf sourd
dear cher
death la mort
decaffeinated sans caféine
December décembre
decide décider
deck le pont
deck chair la chaise longue
deep profond
delay le retard
deliberately exprès
delicious délicieux
demand exiger
dentist le dentiste
dentures le dentier
deodorant le déodorant
department store le grand magasin
departure le départ
depend: it depends ça dépend
depressed déprimé

dessert le dessert
develop développer
device l'appareil *m*
diabetic diabétique
dialect le dialecte
dialling code l'indicatif *m*
diamond le diamant
diarrhoea la diarrhée
diary l'agenda *m*
dictionary le dictionnaire
die mourir
diesel (*fuel*) le gas-oil
diet le régime
different différent
difficult difficile
dining car le wagon-restaurant
dining room la salle à manger
dinner le dîner; **have dinner** dîner
direct direct
direction le sens
directory enquiries les renseignements *mpl*
dirty sale
disabled handicapé
disappear disparaître
disappointed déçu
disaster le désastre
disco la discothèque
disease la maladie
disgusting dégoûtant
disinfectant le désinfectant
distance la distance
distributor le delco
district (*in town*) le quartier
disturb déranger
dive plonger
divorced divorcé
do faire; **that'll do nicely** ça va bien
doctor le médecin

document le document
dog le chien
doll la poupée
donkey l'âne *m*
door la porte
double double
double room la chambre pour deux personnes
down: I feel a bit down j'ai le cafard; **down there** là-bas
downstairs en bas
draught le courant d'air
dream le rêve
dress la robe
dress (*someone*) habiller; (*oneself*) s'habiller
dressing gown la robe de chambre
drink la boisson
drink (*verb*) boire
drinking water l'eau potable *f*
drive conduire
driver le conducteur
driving licence le permis de conduire
drop la goutte
drop (*verb*) laisser tomber
drug (*narcotic*) la drogue
drunk ivre
dry sec, *f* sèche
dry (*verb*) sécher
dry-cleaner le teinturier
duck le canard
durex (*R*) le préservatif
during pendant
dustbin la poubelle
Dutch hollandais
duty-free hors taxes
duty-free shop la boutique hors taxes

ENGLISH-FRENCH

each chaque
ear l'oreille *f*
early tôt; (*too early*) en avance
earrings les boucles d'oreille *fpl*
earth la terre
east l'est *m*; **east of** à l'est de
Easter Pâques
easy facile
eat manger
egg l'oeuf *m*; **hard-boiled egg** oeuf dur; **boiled egg** oeuf à la coque
egg cup le coquetier
either . . . or soit . . . soit . . .
elastic élastique
Elastoplast (*R*) le pansement adhésif
elbow le coude
electric électrique
electricity l'électricité *f*
else: **something else** autre chose
elsewhere ailleurs
embarrassing gênant
embassy l'ambassade *f*
emergency l'urgence *f*
emergency exit la sortie de secours
empty vide
end la fin
engaged (*toilet, phone*) occupé; (*to be married*) fiancé
engine le moteur; (*train*) la locomotive
England l'Angleterre *f*

English anglais; **the English** les Anglais
English girl/ woman l'Anglaise *f*
Englishman l'Anglais *m*
enlargement l'agrandissement *m*
enough assez de; **that's enough** ça suffit
enter entrer dans
entrance l'entrée *f*
envelope l'enveloppe *f*
epileptic épileptique
especially spécialement
Eurocheque l'eurochèque *m*
Europe l'Europe *f*
European européen
even: **even men/ if** même les hommes/ si; **even more beautiful** encore plus beau
evening le soir; **good evening** bonsoir
every chaque; **every time** chaque fois; **every day** tous les jours
everyone tout le monde
everything tout
everywhere partout
exaggerate exagérer
example l'exemple *m*; **for example** par exemple
excellent excellent
except sauf
excess baggage l'excédent de bagages *m*
exchange échanger
exchange rate le cours du change
exciting passionnant
excuse me pardon
exhaust le pot d'échappement
exhibition l'exposition *f*

exit la sortie
expensive cher
explain expliquer
extension lead la rallonge
eye l'oeil *m*, *pl* yeux
eyebrow le sourcil
eyeliner l'eye-liner *m*
eye shadow l'ombre à
  paupières *f*

face le visage
factory l'usine *f*
faint (*verb*) s'évanouir
fair (*funfair*) la foire;
  (*adjective*) juste
fall tomber
false faux
family la famille
famous célèbre
fan le ventilateur
fan belt la courroie du
  ventilateur
far (away) loin
farm la ferme
farmer l'agriculteur *m*
fashion la mode
fashionable à la mode
fast rapide
fat gros, *f* grosse
fat le gras
father le père
father-in-law le beau-père
fault: it's my/ his fault c'est
  de ma/ sa faute
faulty défectueux
favourite préféré
fear la peur
February février

fed up: I'm fed up (with) j'en
  ai marre (de)
feel sentir; **I feel well/
  unwell** je me sens bien/
  mal; **I feel like** j'ai envie de
feeling le sentiment
felt-tip pen le stylo-feutre
feminist féministe
fence la barrière
ferry le ferry-boat; (*small*) le
  bac
fever la fièvre
few: few tourists peu de
  touristes; **a few** quelques-
  uns; **a few ...** quelques ...
fiancé, fiancée le fiancé, la
  fiancée
field le champ
fight la bagarre
fight (*verb*) se battre
fill remplir
fillet le filet
filling (*tooth*) le plombage
film le film
filter le filtre
find trouver
fine l'amende *f*
fine (*weather*) beau
finger le doigt
fingernail l'ongle *m*
finish terminer
fire le feu; (*blaze*) l'incendie *m*
fire brigade les pompiers *mpl*
fire extinguisher
  l'extincteur *m*
fireworks les feux d'artifice
  mpl
first premier
first (*firstly*) d'abord
first aid les premiers secours
  mpl
first class la première
first floor le premier

first name le prénom
fish le poisson
fishbone l'arête f
fishing la pêche
fishmonger's la poissonnerie
fit (*healthy*) en forme
fizzy gazeux
flag le drapeau
flash le flash
flat l'appartement m
flat (*adjective*) plat; (*tyre*) crevé
flavour l'arôme m
flea la puce
flight le vol
flirt flirter
floor (*of room*) le plancher; (*storey*) l'étage m
florist le fleuriste
flour la farine
flower la fleur
flu la grippe
fly la mouche
fly (*verb*) voler
fog le brouillard
folk music la musique folklorique
follow suivre
food la nourriture
food poisoning l'intoxication alimentaire f
foot, *pl* **feet** le pied; **on foot** à pied
football le football
for pour
forbidden défendu
forehead le front
foreign étranger
foreigner l'étranger m
forest la forêt
forget oublier
fork la fourchette; (*in road*) l'embranchement m

form le formulaire
fortnight la quinzaine
fortunately heureusement
forward (*mail*) faire suivre
foundation cream le fond de teint
fountain la fontaine
fracture la fracture
France la France
free libre; (*of charge*) gratuit
freezer le congélateur
French français
French girl/ woman la Française
Frenchman le Français
fresh frais, f fraîche
Friday vendredi
fridge le frigo
friend l'ami m, l'amie f
from: from Plymouth to Inverness de Plymouth à Inverness
front (*part*) l'avant m; **in front of** devant
frost le gel
frozen (*food*) surgelé
fruit les fruits mpl
fry frire
frying pan la poêle
full plein
full board la pension complète
fun: have fun s'amuser
funeral l'enterrement m
funnel (*for pouring*) l'entonnoir m
funny (*strange, amusing*) drôle
furious furieux
furniture les meubles mpl
further plus loin
fuse le fusible
future le futur

G

game (*to play*) le jeu; (*meat*) le gibier
garage le garage
garden le jardin
garlic l'ail *m*
gas le gaz
gas permeable lenses les lentilles semi-rigides *fpl*
gauge la jauge
gay homosexuel
gear la vitesse
gearbox la boîte de vitesses
gear lever le levier de vitesses
gentleman le monsieur
gents (*toilet*) les toilettes pour messieurs *fpl*
genuine authentique
German allemand
Germany l'Allemagne *f*
get obtenir; **can you tell me how to get to ...?** pouvez-vous me dire comment aller à ...?; **get back** (*return*) rentrer; **get in** (*car*) monter; **get off** descendre; **get up** se lever; **get out!** dehors !
gin le gin
gin and tonic le gin-tonic
girl la fille
girlfriend la petite amie
give donner; **give back** rendre
glad content
glass le verre
glasses les lunettes *fpl*
gloves les gants *mpl*
glue la colle

go aller; **go in** entrer; **go out** sortir; **go down** descendre; **go up** monter; **go through** traverser; **go away** partir; **go away!** allez-vous-en !
goat la chèvre
God Dieu *m*
gold l'or *m*
golf le golf
good bon; **good!** bien !
goodbye au revoir
goose l'oie *f*
got: have you got ...? avez-vous ... ?
government le gouvernement
grammar la grammaire
grandfather le grand-père
grandmother la grand-mère
grapefruit le pamplemousse
grapes le raisin
grass l'herbe *f*
grateful reconnaissant
greasy gras
Greece la Grèce
Greek grec
green vert
greengrocer le marchand de légumes
grey gris
grilled grillé
grocer's l'épicerie *f*
ground floor le rez-de-chaussée
group le groupe
guarantee la garantie
guest l'invité *m*
guesthouse la pension
guide le guide
guidebook le guide
guitar la guitare
gun (*rifle*) le fusil; (*pistol*) le pistolet

H

habit l'habitude f
hail (*ice*) la grêle
hair les cheveux mpl
haircut la coupe de cheveux
hairdresser le coiffeur
hair dryer le sèche-cheveux
hair spray la laque
half la moitié; **half a litre/ day** un demi-litre/ une demi-journée; **half an hour** une demi-heure
half board la demi-pension
ham le jambon
hamburger le hamburger
hammer le marteau
hand la main
handbag le sac à main
handbrake le frein à main
handkerchief le mouchoir
handle la poignée
hand luggage les bagages à main mpl
handsome beau
hanger le cintre
hangover la gueule de bois
happen arriver
happy heureux; **happy Christmas!** joyeux Noël !; **happy New Year!** bonne année !
harbour le port
hard dur
hard lenses les lentilles dures fpl
hat le chapeau
hate détester
have avoir (*see grammar*); **I have to ...** je dois ...

hay fever le rhume des foins
hazelnut la noisette
he il
head la tête
headache le mal à la tête
headlights les phares mpl
healthy bon pour la santé
hear entendre
hearing aid l'audiophone m
heart le cœur
heart attack la crise cardiaque
heat la chaleur
heater le radiateur
heating le chauffage
heavy lourd
heel le talon
helicopter l'hélicoptère m
hello bonjour; (*evening*) bonsoir
help l'aide f; **help!** au secours !
help (*verb*) aider
her (*possessive*) son, sa, ses; (*object*) la, elle (*see grammar*)
herbs les fines herbes fpl
here ici; **here is/ are** voilà
hers le sien, la sienne (*see grammar*)
hiccups le hoquet
hide cacher
high haut
highway code le code de la route
hill la colline
him le, lui (*see grammar*)
hip la hanche
hire: for hire à louer
his son, sa, ses; **it's his** c'est le sien/ la sienne (*see grammar*)
history l'histoire f
hit frapper
hitchhike faire du stop

ENGLISH-FRENCH

hitchhiking le stop
hobby le hobby
hold tenir
hole le trou
holiday les vacances *fpl*;
  (public) le jour férié;
  summer holidays les
  grandes vacances
Holland la Hollande
home: at home à la maison;
  go home rentrer à la maison
homemade fait maison
homesick: I'm homesick j'ai
  le mal du pays
honest honnête
honey le miel
honeymoon le voyage de
  noces
hoover (R) l'aspirateur *m*
hope espérer
horn le klaxon
horrible horrible
horse le cheval
horse riding l'équitation *f*
hospital l'hôpital *m*
hospitality l'hospitalité *f*
hot chaud; *(to taste)* piquant
hotel l'hôtel *m*
hot-water bottle la bouillotte
hour l'heure *f*
house la maison
house wine le vin ordinaire
how? comment ?; **how are
  you?** comment allez-vous ?;
  how are things? ça va ?;
  how many/ much?
  combien ?
humour l'humour *m*
hungry: I'm hungry j'ai faim
hurry *(verb)* se dépêcher;
  hurry up! dépêchez-vous !
hurt faire mal
husband le mari

I je
ice la glace
ice cream la glace
ice lolly l'esquimau *m*
idea l'idée *f*
idiot l'idiot *m*
if si
ignition l'allumage *m*
ill malade
immediately immédiatement
important important
impossible impossible
improve améliorer
in dans; **in London** à
  Londres; **in France/ 1945** en
  France/ 1945; **in English** en
  anglais; **is he in?** il est là ?
included compris
incredible incroyable
independent indépendant
indicator *(car)* le clignotant
indigestion l'indigestion *f*
industry l'industrie *f*
infection l'infection *f*
information le
  renseignement
information desk les
  renseignements *mpl*
injection la piqûre
injured blessé
inner tube la chambre à air
innocent innocent
insect l'insecte *m*
insect repellent la crème anti-
  insecte
inside à l'intérieur (de)
insomnia l'insomnie *f*
instant coffee le café soluble
instructor le moniteur

ENGLISH-FRENCH

insurance l'assurance *f*
intelligent intelligent
interesting intéressant
introduce présenter
invitation l'invitation *f*
invite inviter
Ireland l'Irlande *f*
Irish irlandais
iron (*metal*) le fer; (*for clothes*) le fer à repasser
iron (*verb*) repasser
ironmonger's la quincaillerie
island l'île *f*
it ça; **it is ...** c'est ... (*see grammar*)
Italian italien
Italy l'Italie *f*
itch la démangeaison
IUD le stérilet

jack (*car*) le cric
jacket la veste
jam la confiture
January janvier
jaw la mâchoire
jazz le jazz
jealous jaloux
jeans le jean
jellyfish la méduse
jeweller's la bijouterie
jewellery les bijoux *mpl*
Jewish juif, *f* juive
job le travail
jogging le jogging; **go jogging** faire du jogging
joint (*to smoke*) le joint
joke la plaisanterie

journey le voyage
jug le pot
juice le jus
July juillet
jump sauter
jumper le pull
junction le croisement
June juin
just: just two deux seulement

keep garder
kettle la bouilloire
key la clé
kidneys les reins *mpl*; (*to eat*) les rognons *mpl*
kill tuer
kilo le kilo
kilometre le kilomètre
kind aimable
king le roi
kiss le baiser
kiss (*verb*) embrasser
kitchen la cuisine
knee le genou
knife le couteau
knit tricoter
knock over renverser
know savoir; (*person*) connaître; **I don't know** je ne sais pas

label l'étiquette *f*
ladder l'échelle *f*

ladies (*toilet*) les toilettes pour dames *fpl*
lady la dame
lager la bière
lake le lac
lamb l'agneau *m*
lamp la lampe
land (*verb*) atterrir
landscape le paysage
language la langue
language school l'école de langues *f*
large grand
last dernier; **last year** l'année dernière; **at last** enfin
late tard; **arrive/ be late** arriver/ être en retard; **later** plus tard
laugh rire
launderette le lavomatic
laundry (*to wash*) le linge sale; (*place*) la blanchisserie
law la loi
lawn la pelouse
lawyer l'avocat *m*
laxative le laxatif
lazy paresseux
leaf la feuille
leaflet le dépliant
leak la fuite
learn apprendre
least: at least au moins
leather le cuir
leave laisser; (*go away*) partir; (*forget*) oublier
left la gauche; **on the left (of)** à gauche (de)
left-handed gaucher
left luggage la consigne
leg la jambe
lemon le citron
lemonade la limonade
lemon tea le thé citron

lend prêter
length la longueur
lens l'objectif *m*
less moins
lesson la leçon
let (*allow*) laisser
letter la lettre
letterbox la boîte à lettres
lettuce la laitue
level crossing le passage à niveau
library la bibliothèque
licence le permis
lid le couvercle
lie (*say untruth*) mentir
lie down s'étendre
life la vie
lift (*elevator*) l'ascenseur *m*; **give a lift to** emmener
light (*in room*) la lumière; (*on car*) le phare; **have you got a light?** vous avez du feu ?
light (*adjective*) léger; **light blue** bleu clair
light (*verb*) allumer
light bulb l'ampoule *f*
lighter le briquet
lighthouse le phare
light meter le photomètre
like aimer; **I would like** j'aimerais
like (*as*) comme
lip la lèvre
lipstick le rouge à lèvres
liqueur la liqueur
list la liste
listen (to) écouter
litre le litre
litter les ordures *fpl*
little peu; **a little bit (of)** un peu (de)
live vivre; (*in town etc*) habiter

liver le foie
living room le living
lizard le lézard
lobster le homard
lock la serrure
lock (*verb*) fermer à clé
lollipop la sucette
London Londres
long long, *f* longue; **a long time** longtemps
look: look (at) regarder; (*seem*) avoir l'air; **look like** ressembler à; **look for** chercher; **look out!** attention !
lorry le camion
lose perdre
lost property office les objets trouvés *mpl*
lot: a lot (of) beaucoup (de)
loud fort
lounge le salon
love l'amour *m*; **make love** faire l'amour
love (*verb*) aimer
lovely ravissant
low bas
luck la chance; **good luck!** bonne chance !
luggage les bagages *mpl*
lukewarm tiède
lunch le déjeuner
lungs les poumons *mpl*

macho macho
mad fou, *f* folle
Madam madame
magazine le magazine

maiden name le nom de jeune fille
mail le courrier
main principal
make faire
make-up le maquillage
male chauvinist pig le phallocrate
man l'homme *m*
manager le patron
many beaucoup; **many ...** beaucoup de ...
map la carte; (*of town*) le plan
March mars
margarine la margarine
market le marché
marmalade la confiture d'orange
married marié
mascara le mascara
mass la messe
match (*light*) l'allumette *f*; (*sport*) le match
material le tissu
matter: it doesn't matter ça ne fait rien
mattress le matelas
May mai
maybe peut-être
mayonnaise la mayonnaise
me me; **for me** pour moi; **me too** moi aussi (*see grammar*)
meal le repas; **enjoy your meal!** bon appétit !
mean (*verb*) signifier
measles la rougeole; **German measles** la rubéole
meat la viande
mechanic le mécanicien
medicine (*drug*) le médicament
Mediterranean la Méditerranée

medium (*steak*) à point
medium-sized moyen
meet rencontrer
meeting la réunion
melon le melon
mend réparer
menu la carte; **set menu** le menu
mess la pagaille
message le message
metal le métal
metre le mètre
midday midi
middle le milieu
Middle Ages le moyen âge
midnight minuit
milk le lait
minced meat la viande hachée
mind: do you mind if I ...? ça vous dérange si je ... ?
mine le mien, la mienne (*see grammar*)
mineral water l'eau minérale *f*
minute la minute
mirror le miroir
Miss Mademoiselle, Mlle
miss (*train etc*) rater; **I miss you** tu me manques
mistake l'erreur *f*
misunderstanding le malentendu
mix mélanger
modern moderne
moisturizer la crème hydratante
Monday lundi
money l'argent *m*
month le mois
monument le monument
mood l'humeur *f*
moon la lune

moped la mobylette
more plus; **no more ...** plus de ...
morning le matin; **good morning** bonjour
mosquito le moustique
most (of) la plupart (de)
mother la mère
mother-in-law la belle-mère
motorbike la moto
motorboat le hors-bord
motorway l'autoroute *f*
mountain la montagne
mouse la souris
moustache la moustache
mouth la bouche
move (*change position*) bouger
Mr Monsieur, M
Mrs Madame, Mme
Ms Mme, Mlle
much beaucoup; **not much time** pas beaucoup de temps
mum la maman
muscle le muscle
museum le musée
mushrooms les champignons *mpl*
music la musique
musical instrument l'instrument de musique *m*
mussels les moules *fpl*
must: I/ she must je dois/ elle doit
mustard la moutarde
my mon, ma, mes (*see grammar*)

nail (*in wall*) le clou

nail clippers la pince à ongles
nailfile la lime à ongles
nail polish le vernis à ongles
nail polish remover le dissolvant
naked nu
name le nom; **what's your name?** comment vous appelez-vous ?; **my name is Jim** je m'appelle Jim
napkin la serviette
nappy la couche
nappy-liners les protège-couches *mpl*
narrow étroit
nationality la nationalité
natural naturel
nature la nature
near près de; **near here** près d'ici; **the nearest ...** le/ la ... le/ la plus proche
nearly presque
necessary nécessaire
neck le cou
necklace le collier
need: I need ... j'ai besoin de ...
needle l'aiguille *f*
negative *(film)* le négatif
neighbour le voisin, la voisine
neither ... nor ... ni ... ni ...
nephew le neveu
nervous nerveux
neurotic névrosé
never jamais
new nouveau, *f* nouvelle; *(brand-new)* neuf, *f* neuve
news les nouvelles *fpl*
newsagent le tabac-journaux
newspaper le journal
New Year le Nouvel An

next prochain; *(following)* suivant; **next year** l'année prochaine
next to à côté de
nice *(person)* sympathique; *(place)* joli; *(food)* bon
nickname le surnom
niece la nièce
night la nuit; **good night** bonne nuit
nightclub la boîte de nuit
nightdress la chemise de nuit
nightmare le cauchemar
no non; **no ...** pas de ...
nobody personne
noise le bruit
noisy bruyant
non-smoking non-fumeurs
normal normal
north le nord; **north of** au nord de
Northern Ireland l'Irlande du Nord *f*
nose le nez
not pas; **I'm not tired** je ne suis pas fatigué
note *(money)* le billet de banque
notebook le cahier
nothing rien
novel le roman
November novembre
now maintenant
nowhere nulle part
number *(house, phone)* le numéro
number plate la plaque minéralogique
nurse l'infirmière *f*
nut *(to eat)* la noix; *(for bolt)* l'écrou *m*

ENGLISH-FRENCH

obnoxious insupportable
obvious évident
October octobre
octopus le poulpe
of de (*see grammar*)
off (*lights*) éteint
offend blesser
offer offrir
office le bureau
off-licence le marchand de vins
often souvent
oil l'huile *f*
ointment la pommade
OK d'accord; **I'm OK** ça va
old vieux, *f* vieille; **how old are you?** quel âge avez-vous ?; **I'm 25 years old** j'ai 25 ans
old-age pensioner le retraité
olive l'olive *f*
olive oil l'huile d'olive *f*
omelette l'omelette *f*
on sur; (*lights*) allumé
once une fois
one un, *f* une
onion l'oignon *m*
only seulement
open (*adjective*) ouvert
open (*verb*) ouvrir
opera l'opéra *m*
operation l'opération *f*
opposite le contraire
opposite: opposite the church en face de l'église
optician l'opticien *m*
optimistic optimiste
or ou
orange l'orange *f*

orange (*colour*) orange
orchestra l'orchestre *m*
order commander
organize organiser
other autre
otherwise sinon
our notre, nos (*see grammar*)
ours le/la nôtre (*see grammar*)
out: she's out elle est sortie
outside dehors
oven le four
over (*above*) au-dessus de; (*finished*) fini; **over there** là-bas
overdone trop cuit
overtake doubler
owner le propriétaire
oyster l'huître *f*

pack (*verb*) faire ses bagages
package le paquet
package tour le voyage organisé
packed lunch le casse-croûte
packet (*of cigarettes etc*) le paquet
page la page
pain la douleur
painful douloureux
painkiller l'analgésique *m*
paint (*verb*) peindre
paint brush le pinceau
painting le tableau
pair la paire
palace le palais
pancake la crêpe
panic la panique
panties le slip

paper le papier
parcel le colis
pardon? comment ?
parents les parents *mpl*
park le parc
park (*verb*) se garer
part la partie
party (*celebration*) la fête;
   (*group*) le groupe
pass (*mountain*) le col
passenger le passager
passport le passeport
pasta les pâtes *fpl*
pâté le pâté
path le sentier
pavement le trottoir
pay payer
peach la pêche
peanuts les cacahuètes *fpl*
pear la poire
peas les petits pois *mpl*
pedal la pédale
pedestrian le piéton
pedestrian crossing le
   passage clouté
pedestrian precinct la zone
   piétonne
pen le stylo
pencil le crayon
pencil sharpener le taille-
   crayon
penicillin la pénicilline
penis le pénis
penknife le canif
people les gens *mpl*
pepper (*spice*) le poivre;
   (*vegetable*) le poivron
per: per week par semaine;
   per cent pour cent
perfect parfait
perfume le parfum
period la période; (*woman's*)
   les règles *fpl*

perm la permanente
person la personne
petrol l'essence *f*
petrol station la station-
   service
phone (*verb*) téléphoner (à)
phone book l'annuaire *m*
phone box la cabine
   téléphonique
phone number le numéro de
   téléphone
photograph la photographie
photograph (*verb*)
   photographier
photographer le
   photographe
phrase book le manuel de
   conversation
pickpocket le pickpocket
picnic le picnic
pie (*fruit*) la tarte
piece le morceau
pig le cochon
piles les hémorroïdes *fpl*
pill la pilule
pillow l'oreiller *m*
pilot le pilote
pin l'épingle *f*
pineapple l'ananas *m*
pink rose
pipe le tuyau; (*to smoke*) la
   pipe
pity: it's a pity c'est
   dommage
pizza la pizza
plane l'avion *m*
plant la plante
plastic le plastique
plastic bag le sac en plastique
plate l'assiette *f*
platform (*station*) le quai
play (*theatre*) la pièce de
   théâtre

play (*verb*) jouer
pleasant agréable
please s'il vous plaît
pleased content; **pleased to meet you!** enchanté !
pliers la pince
plug (*electrical*) la prise; (*in sink*) la bonde
plum la prune
plumber le plombier
p.m.: 3 p.m. 3 heures de l'après-midi; **11 p.m.** 11 heures du soir
pneumonia la pneumonie
pocket la poche
poison le poison
police la police
policeman l'agent de police *m*
police station le commissariat
polite poli
political politique
politics la politique
polluted pollué
pond l'étang *m*
pony le poney
poor pauvre
pop music la musique pop
pork le porc
port (*drink*) le porto
porter (*hotel*) le portier
possible possible
post (*verb*) poster
postcard la carte postale
poster (*for room*) le poster; (*in street*) l'affiche *f*
poste restante la poste restante
postman le facteur
post office la poste
potato la pomme de terre
poultry la volaille

pound la livre
power cut la coupure de courant
practical pratique
pram le landau
prawn la crevette
prefer préférer
pregnant enceinte
prepare préparer
prescription l'ordonnance *f*
present (*gift*) le cadeau
pretty joli; **pretty good** assez bien
price le prix
priest le prêtre
prince le prince
princess la princesse
printed matter l'imprimé *m*
prison la prison
private privé
probably probablement
problem le problème
programme le programme
prohibited interdit
promise (*verb*) promettre
pronounce prononcer
protect protéger
Protestant protestant; **Protestant church** le temple
proud fier
public public
pull tirer
pump la pompe
puncture la crevaison
punk punk
purple violet
purse le porte-monnaie
push pousser
pushchair la poussette
put mettre
pyjamas le pyjama

Q

quality la qualité
quarter le quart
quay le quai
queen la reine
question la question
queue la queue
queue (*verb*) faire la queue
quick rapide
quickly vite
quiet tranquille; **quiet!**
silence !
quilt le duvet
quite assez

R

rabbit le lapin
radiator le radiateur
radio la radio
railway le chemin de fer
rain la pluie
rain (*verb*) pleuvoir; **it's
raining** il pleut
rainbow l'arc-en-ciel *m*
raincoat l'imperméable *m*
rape le viol
rare rare; (*steak*) bleu
raspberry la framboise
rat le rat
rather plutôt
raw cru
razor le rasoir
razor blade la lame de rasoir
read lire
ready prêt

really vraiment
rear lights les feux arrière *mpl*
rearview mirror le
rétroviseur
receipt le reçu
receive recevoir
reception (*hotel*) la réception
receptionist le/la
réceptionniste
recipe la recette
recognize reconnaître
recommend recommander
record le disque
record player
l'électrophone *m*
record shop le disquaire
red rouge
red-headed roux, *f* rousse
refund rembourser
relax se détendre
religion la religion
remember se souvenir de; **I
remember** je m'en souviens
rent le loyer
rent (*verb*) louer
repair réparer
repeat répéter
reservation la réservation
reserve réserver
responsible responsable
rest (*remaining*) le reste; (*sleep*)
le repos; **take a rest** se
reposer
restaurant le restaurant
return ticket l'aller retour *m*
reverse (*gear*) la marche
arrière
rheumatism les rhumatismes
mpl
rib la côte
rice le riz
rich riche; (*food*) lourd
ridiculous ridicule

right (*side*) la droite; **on the right (of)** à droite (de)
right (*correct*) juste
right of way la priorité
ring (*on finger*) la bague
ring (*phone*) téléphoner à
ripe mûr
river la rivière
road la route; (*in town*) la rue
roadsign le panneau de signalisation
roadworks les travaux *mpl*
rock le rocher
rock climbing la varappe
rock music le rock
roll le petit pain
roof le toit
roof rack la galerie
room la chambre
rope la corde
rose la rose
rosé wine le rosé
rotten pourri
round (*circular*) rond
roundabout le rond-point
route l'itinéraire *m*
rowing boat le bateau à rames
rubber le caoutchouc; (*eraser*) la gomme
rubber band l'élastique *m*
rubbish les ordures *fpl*
rucksack le sac à dos
rude grossier
rug le tapis
ruins les ruines *fpl*
rum le rhum
run courir

sad triste
safe en sécurité
safety pin l'épingle de nourrice *f*
sailboard la planche à voile
sailing la voile
sailing boat le bateau à voile
salad la salade
salad dressing la vinaigrette
sale la vente; (*reduced price*) les soldes *mpl*; **for sale** à vendre
salmon le saumon
salt le sel
salty salé
same même
sand le sable
sandals les sandales *fpl*
sand dunes les dunes *fpl*
sandwich le sandwich
sanitary towel la serviette hygiénique
sardine la sardine
Saturday samedi
sauce la sauce
saucepan la casserole
saucer la soucoupe
sauna le sauna
sausage la saucisse
savoury salé
say dire
Scandinavia la Scandinavie
scarf (*neck*) l'écharpe *f*; (*head*) le foulard
scenery le paysage
school l'école *f*
science la science
scissors les ciseaux *mpl*
Scotland l'Ecosse *f*

Scottish écossais
scrambled eggs les œufs brouillés *mpl*
scream crier
screw la vis
screwdriver le tournevis
sea la mer
seafood les fruits de mer *mpl*
seagull la mouette
seasick: I'm seasick j'ai le mal de mer
seaside: at the seaside au bord de la mer
season la saison; in the high season en haute saison
seat le siège; (*place*) la place
seat belt la ceinture de sécurité
seaweed les algues *fpl*
second (*in time*) la seconde
second-hand d'occasion
secret secret
see voir; see you tomorrow à demain
self-service self-service
sell vendre
sellotape (R) le papier collant
send envoyer
sensible raisonnable
sensitive sensible
separate séparé
separately séparément
September septembre
serious sérieux
serve servir
service le service
service charge le service
serviette la serviette
several plusieurs
sew coudre
sex le sexe
sexist sexiste
sexy sexy

shade l'ombre *f*
shampoo le shampoing
share (*verb*) partager
shark le requin
shave se raser
shaving brush le blaireau
shaving foam la mousse à raser
she elle
sheep le mouton
sheet le drap
shell la coquille
shellfish les crustacés *mpl*
ship le bateau
shirt la chemise
shock le choc
shock-absorber l'amortisseur *m*
shocking scandaleux
shoe laces les lacets *mpl*
shoe polish le cirage
shoe repairer le cordonnier
shoes les chaussures *fpl*
shop le magasin
shopping le shopping; go shopping faire du shopping
shopping bag le cabas
shopping centre le centre commercial
shore le rivage
short court
shortcut le raccourci
shorts les shorts *mpl*
shortsighted myope
shoulder l'épaule *f*
shout crier
show (*verb*) montrer
shower la douche; (*rain*) l'averse *f*
shutter (*photo*) l'obturateur *m*
shutters (*window*) les volets *mpl*

shy timide
sick: **I feel sick** je me sens mal; **I'm going to be sick** j'ai envie de vomir
side le côté
sidelights les feux de position *mpl*
sign signer
silence le silence
silk la soie
silver l'argent *m*
silver foil le papier d'argent
similar semblable
simple simple
since (*time*) depuis (que)
sincere sincère
sing chanter
single (*unmarried*) célibataire
single room la chambre pour une personne
single ticket l'aller simple *m*
sink l'évier *m*
sink (*go under*) couler
sir Monsieur
sister la soeur
sister-in-law la belle-soeur
sit down s'asseoir
size la taille
ski le ski
ski (*verb*) skier
ski boots les chaussures de ski *fpl*
skid déraper
skiing le ski
ski-lift le remonte-pente
skin la peau
skin cleanser le démaquillant
skin-diving la plongée sous-marine
skinny maigre
skirt la jupe
ski slope la piste de ski
skull le crâne

sky le ciel
sleep dormir
sleeper le wagon-lit
sleeping bag le sac de couchage
sleeping pill le somnifère
sleepy: **I'm sleepy** j'ai sommeil
slice la tranche
slide (*photo*) la diapositive
slim mince
slippers les pantoufles *fpl*
slippery glissant
slow lent
slowly lentement
small petit
smell l'odeur *f*
smell (*verb*) sentir
smile le sourire
smile (*verb*) sourire
smoke la fumée
smoke (*verb*) fumer
smoking (*compartment*) fumeurs
snack le casse-croûte
snail l'escargot *m*
snake le serpent
sneeze éternuer
snore ronfler
snow la neige
so: **so beautiful/ big** si beau/ grand
soaking solution la solution de trempage
soap le savon
society la société
socket la prise
socks les chaussettes *fpl*
soft doux, *f* douce
soft drink la boisson non-alcoolisée
soft lenses les lentilles souples *fpl*

81

sole (*of shoe*) la semelle

some quelques-uns; **some wine/ flour/ biscuits** du vin/ de la farine/ des biscuits

somebody quelqu'un

something quelque chose

sometimes parfois

somewhere quelque part

son le fils

song la chanson

son-in-law le beau-fils

soon bientôt

sore: I've got a sore throat j'ai mal à la gorge

sorry excusez-moi; **I'm sorry** je suis désolé

soup le potage

sour acide

south le sud; **south of** au sud de

souvenir le souvenir

spade la pelle

Spain l'Espagne *f*

Spanish espagnol

spanner la clé anglaise

spare parts les pièces de rechange *fpl*

spare tyre le pneu de rechange

spark plug la bougie

speak parler; **do you speak...?** parlez-vous ... ?

speciality la spécialité

speed la vitesse

speed limit la limitation de vitesse

speedometer le compteur

spend dépenser

spice l'épice *f*

spider l'araignée *f*

spinach les épinards *mpl*

spoke le rayon

spoon la cuiller

sport le sport

spot (*on skin*) le bouton

sprain: I sprained my ankle je me suis foulé la cheville

spring (*season*) le printemps; (*in seat etc*) le ressort

square (*in town*) la place

stain la tache

stairs l'escalier *m*

stamp le timbre

stand: I can't stand cheese je ne supporte pas le fromage

star l'étoile *f*

starter (*food*) l'entrée *f*

state l'état *m*

station la gare

stationer's la papeterie

stay le séjour

stay (*remain*) rester; (*in hotel etc*) loger

steak le steak

steal voler

steamer le bateau à vapeur

steep raide

steering la direction

steering wheel le volant

stepfather le beau-père

stepmother la belle-mère

steward le steward

stewardess l'hôtesse de l'air *f*

still (*adverb*) encore

sting piquer

stockings les bas *mpl*

stomach le ventre

stomach ache les maux d'estomac *mpl*

stone la pierre

stop l'arrêt *m*

stop s'arrêter; **stop!** arrêtez !

storm la tempête

story l'histoire *f*

straight ahead tout droit

strange (*odd*) bizarre

strawberry la fraise
stream le ruisseau
street la rue
string la ficelle
stroke (*attack*) l'attaque *f*
strong fort
stuck coincé
student l'étudiant *m*, l'étudiante *f*
stupid stupide
suburbs la banlieue
success le succès
suddenly tout d'un coup
suede le daim
sugar le sucre
suit le complet
suit: blue suits you le bleu vous va bien
suitcase la valise
summer l'été *m*
sun le soleil
sunbathe se bronzer
sunblock l'écran total *m*
sunburn le coup de soleil
Sunday dimanche
sunglasses les lunettes de soleil *fpl*
sunny ensoleillé
sunset le coucher de soleil
sunshine le soleil
sunstroke l'insolation *f*
suntan le bronzage
suntan lotion le lait solaire
suntan oil l'huile solaire *f*
supermarket le supermarché
supplement le supplément
sure sûr
surf le surf
surname le nom de famille
surprise la surprise
surprising surprenant
swallow avaler
sweat transpirer

sweater le pullover
sweet le bonbon
sweet (*to taste*) doux, *f* douce
swim nager
swimming la natation; **go swimming** aller se baigner
swimming costume le maillot de bain
swimming pool la piscine
swimming trunks le slip de bain
Swiss suisse
switch l'interrupteur *m*
switch off (*light, television*) éteindre; (*engine*) arrêter
switch on (*light, television*) allumer; (*engine*) mettre en marche
Switzerland la Suisse
swollen enflé
synagogue la synagogue

table la table
tablecloth la nappe
tablet le comprimé
table tennis le ping-pong
tail la queue
take prendre; **take away** (*remove*) enlever; **to take away** (*food*) à emporter; **take off** (*plane*) décoller
talcum powder le talc
talk parler
tall grand
tampon le tampon
tan (*colour*) le bronzage
tank le réservoir
tap le robinet

tape (*cassette*) la bande magnétique
tart la tarte
taste le goût
taste (*try*) goûter
taxi le taxi
tea le thé
teach enseigner
teacher le professeur
team l'équipe *f*
teapot la théière
tea towel le torchon à vaisselle
teenager l'adolescent *m*, l'adolescente *f*
telegram le télégramme
telephone le téléphone
telephone directory le bottin
television la télévision
temperature la température
tennis le tennis
tent la tente
terrible épouvantable
terrific fantastique
than: uglier than plus laid que
thank remercier
thank you merci
that (*adjective*) ce, cette; (*pronoun*) ça, cela; I think that ... je pense que ...; that one celui-là, celle-là
the le, *f* la, *pl* les (*see grammar*)
theatre le théâtre
their leur (*see grammar*)
theirs le/la leur (*see grammar*)
them (*direct object*) les; (*indirect*) leur; (*after preposition*) eux, elles (*see grammar*)
then alors
there là; there is/are il y a; is/are there ...? est-ce qu'il

y a ... ?
thermometer le thermomètre
thermos flask le thermos
these (*adjective*) ces; (*pronoun*) ceux-ci, celles-ci
they ils, *f* elles
thick épais
thief le voleur
thigh la cuisse
thin mince
thing la chose
think penser
thirsty: I'm thirsty j'ai soif
this (*adjective*) ce, cette; (*pronoun*) ceci; this one celui-ci, celle-ci
those (*adjective*) ces; (*pronoun*) ceux-là, celles-là
thread le fil
throat la gorge
throat pastilles les pastilles pour la gorge *fpl*
through par
throw lancer; throw away jeter
thunder le tonnerre
thunderstorm l'orage *m*
Thursday jeudi
ticket le billet
ticket office le guichet
tide la marée
tie la cravate
tight étroit
tights les collants *mpl*
time le temps; (*occasion*) la fois; on time à l'heure; what time is it? quelle heure est-il ?
timetable l'horaire *m*
tin opener l'ouvre-boîte *m*
tip le pourboire
tired fatigué
tissues les kleenex *mpl* (R)

ENGLISH-FRENCH

to: I'm going to Paris/ Scotland je vais à Paris/ en Ecosse
toast le toast
tobacco le tabac
today aujourd'hui
toe l'orteil *m*
together ensemble
toilet les toilettes *fpl*
toilet paper le papier hygiénique
tomato la tomate
tomorrow demain
tongue la langue
tonight ce soir
tonsillitis l'angine *f*
too (*also*) aussi; **too big** trop grand; **not too much** pas trop
tool l'outil *m*
tooth la dent
toothache le mal de dents
toothbrush la brosse à dents
toothpaste le dentifrice
top: at the top en haut
torch la lampe de poche
touch toucher
tourist le touriste
towel la serviette de bain
tower la tour
town la ville
town hall la mairie
toy le jouet
tracksuit le survêtement de sport
tradition la tradition
traditional traditionnel
traffic la circulation
traffic jam l'embouteillage *m*
traffic lights les feux de signalisation *mpl*
traffic warden le/la contractuel

trailer (*behind car*) la remorque
train le train
trainers les tennis *fpl*
translate traduire
travel voyager
travel agent's l'agence de voyages *f*
traveller's cheque le chèque de voyage
tray le plateau
tree l'arbre *m*
tremendous super
trip l'excursion *f*
trolley le chariot
trousers le pantalon
true vrai
try essayer; **try on** essayer
T-shirt le T-shirt
Tuesday mardi
tuna fish le thon
tunnel le tunnel
turkey la dinde
turn (*verb*) tourner
tweezers la pince à épiler
twins les jumeaux *mpl*
typewriter la machine à écrire
tyre le pneu

U

ugly laid
umbrella le parapluie
uncle l'oncle *m*
under sous
underdone mal cuit
underground le métro
underneath dessous; **underneath ... sous ...**
underpants le slip

ENGLISH-FRENCH

understand comprendre
underwear les sous-
vêtements *mpl*
unemployed au chômage
unfortunately
malheureusement
United States les Etats-Unis
mpl
university l'université *f*
unpack défaire sa valise
unpleasant désagréable
until jusqu'à (ce que)
up: up there là-haut
upstairs en haut
urgent urgent
us nous (*see grammar*)
use utiliser
useful utile
usual habituel
usually d'habitude

vaccination le vaccin
vacuum cleaner
l'aspirateur *m*
vagina le vagin
valid valable
valley la vallée
valve la valve
van la camionnette
vanilla la vanille
vase le vase
VD la maladie vénérienne
veal le veau
vegetables les légumes *mpl*
vegetarian végétarien
vehicle le véhicule
very très; **very much**
beaucoup
vet le vétérinaire

video la vidéo
video recorder le
magnétoscope
view la vue
viewfinder le viseur
villa la villa
village le village
vinegar le vinaigre
vineyard le vignoble
visa le visa
visit la visite
visit (*verb*) visiter
vitamins les vitamines *fpl*
voice la voix

waist la taille
wait attendre
waiter le garçon
waiting room la salle
d'attente
waitress la serveuse
wake up (*someone*) réveiller;
(*oneself*) se réveiller
Wales le Pays de Galles
walk la promenade; **go for a**
walk aller se promener
walk (*verb*) marcher
walkman (*R*) le walkman (*R*)
wall le mur
wallet le portefeuille
want vouloir; **I want** je veux
do you want ...? voulez-
vous ... ?
war la guerre
warm chaud; **it's warm** il fait
chaud
wash laver; (*oneself*) se laver
washbasin le lavabo
washing la lessive

86

washing machine la machine
à laver
washing powder la lessive
washing-up la vaisselle
washing-up liquid le produit
vaisselle
wasp la guêpe
watch (*for time*) la montre
watch (*verb*) regarder
water l'eau *f*
waterfall la cascade
waterski le ski nautique
wave (*in sea*) la vague
way: this way (*like this*)
comme ceci; **can you tell me
the way to ...?** pouvez-
vous m'indiquer comment
aller à ... ?
we nous
weak faible
weather le temps; **the
weather's good** il fait beau
weather forecast la météo
wedding le mariage
Wednesday mercredi
week la semaine
weekend le week-end
weight le poids
welcome! bienvenue !
well: he's well/ not well il va
bien/ mal
well (*adverb*) bien
well done bien cuit
wellingtons les bottes de
caoutchouc *fpl*
Welsh gallois
west l'ouest *m*; **west of** à
l'ouest de
wet mouillé
what ...? que ... ?; **what?**
quoi ?; **what's this?**
qu'est-ce que c'est ?
wheel la roue

wheelchair le fauteuil roulant
when quand
where où
which quel
while pendant que
whipped cream la crème
Chantilly
whisky le whisky
white blanc, *f* blanche
who qui
whole entier
whooping cough la
coqueluche
whose: whose is this? c'est à
qui ?
why pourquoi
wide large
widow la veuve
widower le veuf
wife la femme
wild sauvage
win gagner
wind le vent
window la fenêtre
windscreen le pare-brise
windscreen wiper l'essuie-
glace *m*
wine le vin; **red/ white/ rosé
wine** le vin rouge/ blanc/
rosé
wine list la carte des vins
wing l'aile *f*
winter l'hiver *m*
wire le fil de fer
wish: best wishes meilleurs
voeux
with avec
without sans
witness le témoin
woman la femme
wonderful merveilleux
wood le bois
wool la laine

word le mot
work le travail
work (*verb*) travailler; **it's not working** ça ne marche pas
world le monde
worry le souci
worry about se faire du souci pour
worse pire
worst le/la pire
wound la blessure
wrap emballer
wrapping paper le papier d'emballage
wrench la clé anglaise
wrist le poignet
write écrire
writing paper le papier à lettres
wrong faux

young jeune; **young people** les jeunes
your (*familiar*) ton, ta, tes; (*plural or polite*) votre, vos (*see grammar*)
yours (*familiar*) le tien, la tienne; (*plural or polite*) le/la vôtre (*see grammar*)
youth hostel l'auberge de jeunesse *f*

zero zéro
zip la fermeture éclair
zoo le zoo

X-ray la radio

yacht le yacht
year l'année *f*
yellow jaune
yes oui; **oh yes I do!** mais si!
yesterday hier
yet: not yet pas encore
yoghurt le yaourt
you (*familiar*) tu; (*object*) te; (*after preposition*) toi; (*plural or polite*) vous (*see grammar*)

à: à la gare at the station; à Londres in London; je vais à Paris/ la gare I'm going to Paris/ the station; à 3 heures at 3 o'clock; à demain see you tomorrow; à la vôtre ! cheers!
abeille f bee
abricot m apricot
accélérateur m accelerator
accent m accent
accepter accept
accident m accident
accompagner accompany
acheter buy
acide sour
adaptateur m adaptor
addition f bill
adolescent m teenager
adresse f address
adulte m adult
aéroport m airport
affaires fpl business
affiche f poster
affreux awful
after-shave m aftershave
âge m age; quel âge avez-vous ? how old are you?
agence f agency
agence de voyages f travel agent's
agenda m diary
agent de police m policeman
agneau m lamb

agrandissement m enlargement
agréable pleasant
agressif aggressive
agriculteur m farmer
aide f help
aider help
aiguille f needle
ail m garlic
aile f wing
ailleurs elsewhere
aimable kind
aimer like; love; j'aimerais I would like
air m air; avoir l'air look
alarme f alarm
alcool m alcohol
algues fpl seaweed
allaiter breastfeed
Allemagne f Germany
allemand German
aller go; il va bien/ mal he's well/ not well; allez-vous-en ! go away!; le bleu me va bien blue suits me
allergique à allergic to
aller retour m return ticket
aller simple m single ticket
allumage m ignition
allumer light; switch on
allumette f match
alors then; alors ! well
alternateur m alternator
ambassade f embassy
ambulance f ambulance
améliorer improve
amende f fine
amer bitter

américain American
Amérique f America
ami m, **amie** f friend; **petit ami** boyfriend; **petite amie** girlfriend
amortisseur m shock-absorber
amour m love; **faire l'amour** make love
ampoule f light bulb; blister
amuser: s'amuser have fun
an m year; **j'ai 25 ans** I'm 25 years old
analgésique m painkiller
ananas m pineapple
ancêtre m ancestor
ancien ancient
ancre f anchor
âne m donkey
angine f tonsillitis
angine de poitrine f angina
anglais English
Anglais m, **Anglaise** f Englishman, f English woman; **les Anglais** the English
Angleterre f England
animal m animal
année f year
anniversaire m birthday; **bon anniversaire !** happy birthday!
anniversaire de mariage m wedding anniversary
annuaire m phone book
annuler cancel
anorak m anorak
antibiotique m antibiotic
antigel m antifreeze
antihistaminique m antihistamine
anti-insecte: la crème anti-insecte insect repellent

antiquaire m antique shop
août August
apéritif m aperitif
appareil m device
appareil-photo m camera
appartement m flat
appartenir belong
appeler call; **comment vous appelez-vous ?** what's your name?; **je m'appelle Jim** my name is Jim
appendicite f appendicitis
appétit m appetite; **bon appétit !** enjoy your meal!
apporter bring
apprendre learn
après after
après-demain the day after tomorrow
après-midi m afternoon
arabe Arabic
araignée f spider
arbre m tree
arc-en-ciel m rainbow
archéologie f archaeology
arête f fishbone
argent m money; silver
armoire f cupboard
arôme m flavour
arrêt m stop
arrêt d'autobus m bus stop
arrêter arrest; **s'arrêter** stop; **arrêtez !** stop!
arrière m back
arrière: la roue/ le siège arrière the back wheel/ seat
arrivée f arrival
arriver arrive; happen
art m art
artificiel artificial
artisanat m crafts
artiste m/f artist
ascenseur m lift

asperges *fpl* asparagus
aspirateur *m* hoover (R)
aspirine *f* aspirin
asseoir: s'asseoir sit down
assez (de) enough; quite
assiette *f* plate
assurance *f* insurance
asthme *m* asthma
astucieux clever
Atlantique *m* Atlantic
attaque *f* attack; stroke
attendre wait; **attendez-moi !** wait for me!
attention ! look out!; **faites attention !** be careful!
atterrir land
attraper catch
auberge de jeunesse *f* youth hostel
aubergine *f* aubergine
au-dessus de above
audiophone *m* hearing aid
aujourd'hui today
au revoir goodbye
au secours ! help!
aussi also; **moi aussi** me too; **aussi beau que** as beautiful as
Australie *f* Australia
australien Australian
authentique genuine
autobus *m* bus
automatique automatic
automne *m* autumn
automobile *f* car
automobiliste *m* car driver
autoroute *f* motorway
autostop *m* hitchhiking; **faire du stop** hitchhike
autre other; **un/ une autre** another; **autre chose** something else

Autriche *f* Austria
autrichien Austrian
avaler swallow
avance: d'avance in advance; **en avance** early
avant before
avant *m* front
avant-hier the day before yesterday
avec with
averse *f* shower
aveugle blind
avion *m* plane; **par avion** by airmail
avocat *m* lawyer
avoir have
avril April

B

baby-sitter *m/f* baby-sitter
bac *m* ferry
bagages *mpl* luggage; **bagages à main** hand luggage; **faire ses bagages** pack
bagarre *f* fight
bague *f* ring
baigner: se baigner go swimming
baignoire *f* bathtub
bain *m* bath
baiser *m* kiss
balai *m* broom
balcon *m* balcony
balle *f* ball
ballon *m* ball
banane *f* banana
bande magnétique *f* tape
banlieue *f* suburbs

banque f bank
bar m bar
barbe f beard
barbecue m barbecue
barman m barman
barrière f fence
bas low
bas mpl stockings
bateau m boat
bateau à rames m rowing boat
bateau à vapeur m steamer
bateau à voile m sailing boat
bâtiment m building
batterie f battery
battre: se battre fight
baume après-shampoing m conditioner
beau, f belle beautiful; **il fait beau** the weather is good
beaucoup a lot; **beaucoup de sucre** a lot of sugar
beau-fils m son-in-law
beau-père m father-in-law
bébé m baby
beige beige
belge Belgian
Belgique f Belgium
belle beautiful
belle-fille f daughter-in-law
belle-mère f mother-in-law
béquilles fpl crutches
besoin: j'ai besoin de ... I need ...
bête stupid
beurre m butter
bibliothèque f library
bicyclette f bicycle
bien well; **très bien !** good!
bien que although
bien sûr of course
bientôt soon
bienvenue ! welcome!

bière f beer
bijouterie f jeweller's
bijoux mpl jewellery
bikini m bikini
billet m ticket
billet de banque m banknote
bizarre strange
blaireau m shaving brush
blanc, f blanche white
blanchisserie f laundry
blessé injured
blessure f wound
bleu blue; rare
bleu m bruise
blond blond
boeuf m beef
boire drink
bois m wood
boisson f drink
boîte f box; can
boîte à lettres f letterbox
boîte de nuit f nightclub
boîte de vitesses f gearbox
bol m bowl
bombe f bomb
bon good
bonbon m sweet
bonde f plug
bondé crowded
bonjour hello
bon marché cheap
bonnet de bain m bathing cap
bonsoir good evening
bord m edge; **au bord de la mer** at the seaside
botte f boot
bottes de caoutchouc fpl wellingtons
bottin m telephone directory
bouche f mouth
bouché blocked
boucherie f butcher's

FRENCH-ENGLISH

boucles d'oreille *fpl* earrings
bouée *f* buoy
bouger move
bougie *f* candle; spark plug
bouillir boil
bouillotte *f* hot-water bottle
boulangerie *f* baker's
boussole *f* compass
bouteille *f* bottle
boutique hors taxes *f* duty-free shop
bouton *m* button; spot
bracelet *m* bracelet
bras *m* arm
brique *f* brick
briquet *m* lighter
britannique British
broche *f* brooch
bronzage *m* suntan
bronzer tan; **se bronzer** sunbathe
brosse *f* brush
brosse à dents *f* toothbrush
brouillard *m* fog
bruit *m* noise
brûler burn
brûlure *f* burn
brun brown
brushing *m* blow-dry
bruyant noisy
bureau *m* office
butagaz *m* Calor gas (R)

ça it; that; **ça va ?** how are things?; **ça va** I'm OK
cabas *m* shopping bag
cabine *f* cabin

cabine téléphonique *f* phone box
cacahuètes *fpl* peanuts
cacao *m* cocoa
cacher hide
cadeau *m* present
cafard *m* cockroach; **j'ai le cafard** I feel a bit down
café *m* coffee; café; **café crème** white coffee; **café soluble** instant coffee
caféine *f*: **sans caféine** decaffeinated
cahier *m* notebook
caisse *f* cash desk
calculette *f* calculator
calendrier *m* calendar
calmer: se calmer calm down
caméra *f* camera
camion *m* lorry
camionnette *f* van
campagne *f* countryside
camping *m* camping; campsite
Canada *m* Canada
canadien Canadian
canal *m* canal
canard *m* duck
canif *m* penknife
canoë *m* canoe
caoutchouc *m* rubber
capitaine *m* captain
capot *m* bonnet
car *m* coach
caravane *f* caravan
carburateur *m* carburettor
carnet d'adresses *m* address book
carotte *f* carrot
carte *f* card; map; menu
carte de crédit *f* credit card
carte d'embarquement *f* boarding pass

93

carte des vins *f* wine list
carte de visite *f* card
carte d'identité *f* ID card
carte d'identité bancaire *f*
  cheque card
carte postale *f* postcard
carton *m* box; cardboard
cascade *f* waterfall
casquette *f* cap
cassé broken
casse-croûte *m* snack
casser break
casserole *f* saucepan
cassette *f* cassette
cathédrale *f* cathedral
catholique Catholic
cauchemar *m* nightmare
cause *f* cause; **à cause de**
  because of
ce this; **ce que** what
ceci this
ceinture *f* belt
ceinture de sécurité *f* seat
  belt
cela that
célèbre famous
célibataire single
célibataire *m* bachelor
celui-ci, celle-ci this one
celui-là, celle-là that one
cendrier *m* ashtray
centigrade centigrade
centre *m* centre
centre commercial *m*
  shopping centre
centre-ville *m* city centre
cerise *f* cherry
certificat *m* certificate
ces these
c'est it is
cette this
ceux-ci these
ceux-là those

chaîne *f* chain
chaise *f* chair
chaise longue *f* deck chair
chaleur *f* heat
chambre *f* room; **chambre
  pour une personne/ deux
  personnes** single/ double
  room
chambre à air *f* inner tube
chambre à coucher *f*
  bedroom
champ *m* field
champignons *mpl*
  mushrooms
chance *f* luck; **bonne
  chance !** good luck!
changer change; **se changer**
  change; **changer de train**
  change trains
chanson *f* song
chanter sing
chapeau *m* hat
chaque each
chariot *m* trolley
charter *m* charter flight
chat *m* cat
château *m* castle
chaud hot
chauffage *m* heating
chauffage central *m* central
  heating
chaussettes *fpl* socks
chaussures *fpl* shoes
chaussures de ski *fpl* ski boots
chauve bald
chemin *m* path
chemin de fer *m* railway
chemise *f* shirt
chemise de nuit *f* nightdress
chemisier *m* blouse
chèque *m* cheque
chèque de voyage *m*
  traveller's cheque

chéquier m cheque book
cher dear; expensive
chercher look for
cheval m horse
cheveux mpl hair
cheville f ankle
chèvre f goat
chewing-gum m chewing gum
chez: chez Betty at Betty's; **chez moi** at my place, at home
chien m dog
chips fpl crisps
choc m shock
chocolat m chocolate; **chocolat au lait/ à croquer** milk/ plain chocolate; **chocolat chaud** hot chocolate
choisir choose
chômage m: **au chômage** unemployed
chose f thing
chou m cabbage
chou à la crème m cream puff
chou-fleur m cauliflower
choux de Bruxelles mpl Brussels sprouts
cidre m cider
ciel m sky
cigare m cigar
cigarette f cigarette
cimetière m cemetery
cinéma m cinema
cintre m coathanger
cirage m shoe polish
circulation f traffic
ciseaux mpl scissors
citron m lemon
clair clear; **bleu clair** light blue
classe f class
clé f key

clé anglaise f wrench
clignotant m indicator
climat m climate
climatisation f air-conditioning
climatisé air-conditioned
cloche f bell
clou m nail
club m club
cochon m pig
cocktail m cocktail
code de la route m highway code
coeur m heart
coffre m boot
cognac m brandy
coiffeur m, **coiffeuse** f hairdresser
coin m corner
coincé stuck
col m collar; pass
colis m parcel
collants mpl tights
colle f glue
collection f collection
collier m necklace
colline f hill
collision f crash
combien ? how many?; how much?
commander order
comme like; as
commencer begin
comment ? how?; pardon?
commissariat m police station
compagnie aérienne f airline
compartiment m compartment
complet m suit; full
compliment m compliment
compliqué complicated
comprendre understand

comprimé *m* tablet

compris included; **tout compris** all inclusive

comptant: **payer comptant** pay cash

compteur *m* speedometer

concert *m* concert

concessionnaire *m* agent

concombre *m* cucumber

conducteur *m* driver

conduire drive

confirmer confirm

confiture *f* jam; **confiture d'orange** marmalade

confortable comfortable

congélateur *m* freezer

connaître know

conseiller advise

consigne *f* left luggage

constipé constipated

consulat *m* consulate

contacter contact

content pleased

contraceptif *m* contraceptive

contractuel *m* traffic warden

contraire *m* opposite

contre against

copain *m* chum

coqueluche *f* whooping cough

coquetier *m* egg cup

coquillage *m* shell

corde *f* rope

cordonnier *m* cobbler

corps *m* body

correct correct

correspondance *f* connection

corridor *m* corridor

côte *f* coast; rib

côté *m* side; **à côté de** next to

côtelette *f* chop

coton *m* cotton

coton hydrophile *m* cotton wool

cou *m* neck

couche *f* nappy

coucher: **aller se coucher** go to bed

coucher de soleil *m* sunset

couchette *f* couchette

coude *m* elbow

coudre sew

couler sink

couleur *f* colour

coup *m* blow; **tout à coup** suddenly

coup de soleil *m* sunburn

coupe de cheveux *f* haircut

couper cut

coupure de courant *f* power cut

courageux brave

courant d'air *m* draught

courir run

courrier *m* mail

courroie du ventilateur *f* fan belt

cours du change *m* exchange rate

court short

cousin *m*, cousine *f* cousin

couteau *m* knife

coûter cost

coutume *f* custom

couvercle *m* lid

couverts *mpl* cutlery

couverture *f* blanket

crabe *m* crab

crampe *f* cramp

crâne *m* skull

cravate *f* tie

crayon *m* pencil

crème *f* cream

crème *m* white coffee

crème Chantilly *f* whipped cream

FRENCH-ENGLISH

crème de beauté *f* cold cream
crème démaquillante *f* cleansing cream
crème hydratante *f* moisturizer
crêpe *f* pancake
crevaison *f* puncture
crevette *f* prawn
cric *m* jack
crier scream
crise cardiaque *f* heart attack
croire believe
croisement *m* junction
croisière *f* cruise
cru raw
crustacés *mpl* shellfish
cuiller *f* spoon
cuir *m* leather
cuire cook; bake
cuisine *f* kitchen
cuisinier *m* cook
cuisinière *f* cooker
cuit: trop cuit overdone; mal cuit underdone; bien cuit well done
curry *m* curry
cyclisme *m* cycling
cycliste *m/f* cyclist

d'abord first
d'accord OK; je suis d'accord I agree
daim *m* suede
dame *f* lady
danger *m* danger
dangereux dangerous
dans in
danser dance

date *f* date
de of; la voiture des propriétaires the owners' car; de Plymouth à Inverness from Plymouth to Inverness; du vin/ de la farine/ des biscuits (some) wine/ flour/ biscuits; avez-vous du beurre/ des bananes ? have you got any butter/ bananas?
début *m* beginning
débutant *m* beginner
décembre December
décider decide
décoller take off
déçu disappointed
défaire: défaire sa valise unpack
défectueux faulty
défendu forbidden
dégâts *mpl* damage
dégoûtant disgusting
dehors outside; dehors ! get out!
déjà already
déjeuner *m* lunch
delco *m* distributor
délicieux delicious
demain tomorrow
demander ask (for)
démangeaison *f* itch
démaquillant *m* skin cleanser
demi: un demi-litre/ une demi-journée half a litre/ day; une demi-heure half an hour
demi-pension *f* half board
dent *f* tooth
dentier *m* dentures
dentifrice *m* toothpaste

dentiste *m* dentist
déodorant *m* deodorant
départ *m* departure
dépêcher: se dépêcher hurry;
  dépêchez-vous ! hurry up!
dépendre: ça dépend it
  depends
dépenser spend
dépliant *m* leaflet
dépression *f* nervous
  breakdown
déprimé depressed
depuis (que) since
déranger disturb; **ça vous
  dérange si ... ?** do you
  mind if ...?
déraper skid
dernier last; **l'année
  dernière** last year
derrière *m* bottom
derrière behind
des (*see DE and grammar*)
désagréable unpleasant
désastre *m* disaster
descendre go down; get off
désinfectant *m* disinfectant
désolé: je suis désolé I'm
  sorry
dessert *m* dessert
dessous underneath
détendre: se détendre relax
détester hate
devant in front of
développer develop
devenir become
devoir: je dois/ il doit I/ he
  must
d'habitude usually
diabétique diabetic
dialecte *m* dialect
diamant *m* diamond
diapositive *f* slide
diarrhée *f* diarrhoea

dictionnaire *m* dictionary
Dieu *m* God
différent different
difficile difficult
dimanche Sunday
dinde *f* turkey
dîner *m* dinner
dîner have dinner
dire say
direct direct
direction *f* direction; steering
discothèque *f* disco
disparaître disappear
disquaire *m* record shop
disque *m* record
disque compact *m* compact
  disc
dissolvant *m* nail-polish
  remover
distance *f* distance
distribanque *m* cash
  dispenser
divorcé divorced
docteur *m* doctor
document *m* document
doigt *m* finger
dommage: c'est dommage
  it's a pity
donner give
dont whose
dormir sleep
dos *m* back
douane *f* customs
double double
doubler overtake
douche *f* shower
douleur *f* pain
douloureux painful
doux, *f* douce soft; sweet
drap *m* sheet; **les draps de
  lit** bed linen
drapeau *m* flag
drogue *f* drug

droit straight; **tout droit** straight ahead
droite f right; **à droite (de)** on the right (of)
drôle funny
du (*see DE and grammar*)
dunes fpl **sand dunes**
dur hard
duvet m quilt

eau f water; **eau potable** drinking water
eau de Javel f bleach
eau de toilette f eau de toilette
eau minérale f mineral water
échanger exchange
écharpe f scarf
échelle f ladder
école f school
école de langues f language school
écossais Scottish
Ecosse f Scotland
écouter listen (to)
écrire write
écrou m nut
église f church
élastique m rubber band
élastique elastic
électricité f electricity
électrique electric
électrophone m record player
elle she; her
elles they; them
emballer wrap
embouteillage m traffic jam
embranchement m fork

embrasser kiss
embrayage m clutch
emmener give a lift to
emporter take
emprunter borrow
en: en France/ 1945/ anglais in France/ 1945/ English; **je vais en France** I'm going to France; **en voiture** by car
en bas downstairs
en haut upstairs
enceinte pregnant
enchanté ! pleased to meet you!
encore! again; still; **encore une bière** another beer; **encore plus beau** even more beautiful; **pas encore** not yet
endommager damage
endormi asleep
en face de opposite
enfant m child
enfin at last
enflé swollen
enlever take away
ennuyeux annoying; boring
enregistrement des bagages m check-in
enrhumé: je suis enrhumé I've got a cold
enseignant m teacher
enseigner teach
ensemble together
ensoleillé sunny
ensuite afterwards
entendre hear
enterrement m funeral
entier whole
entonnoir m funnel
entre between
entrée f entrance; starter
entremets m dessert

entrer go in; **entrez !** come in!
enveloppe f envelope
envie f: **j'ai envie de** I feel like
environ about
envoyer send
épais thick
épaule f shoulder
épice f spice
épicerie f grocer's
épileptique epileptic
épinards mpl spinach
épingle f pin
épingle de nourrice f safety pin
épouse f wife
épouvantable terrible
équipage m crew
équipe f team
équitation f horse riding
erreur f mistake
escalier m stairs
escargot m snail
Espagne f Spain
espagnol Spanish
espérer hope
esquimau m ice lolly
essayer try; try on
essence f petrol
essieu m axle
essuie-glace m windscreen wiper
est m east; **à l'est de** east of
estomac m stomach
et and
étage m floor
étang m pond
état m state
Etats-Unis mpl United States
été m summer
éteindre switch off
étendre: s'étendre stretch; lie down

éternuer sneeze
étiquette f label
étoile f star
étonnant astonishing
étranger m foreigner; **à l'étranger** abroad
étranger foreign
être be
étroit narrow; tight
étudiant m, **étudiante** f student
eurochèque m Eurocheque
Europe f Europe
européen European
eux them
évanouir: s'évanouir faint
évident obvious
évier m sink
exagérer exaggerate
excédent de bagages m excess baggage
excellent excellent
excursion f trip
excuser: s'excuser apologize; **excusez-moi** sorry
exemple m example; **par exemple** for example
exiger demand
expliquer explain
exposition f exhibition
exprès deliberately; **par exprès** special delivery
extincteur m fire extinguisher
eye-liner m eyeliner

fâché angry
facile easy
facteur m postman

faible weak
faim f: **j'ai faim** I'm hungry
faire do; make; **ça ne fait rien** it doesn't matter
falaise f cliff
falloir: il faut que je/ vous ... I/ you must ...
famille f family
farine f flour
fatigué tired
fauché: je suis fauché I'm broke
faute f: **c'est de ma/ sa faute** it's my/ his fault
fauteuil roulant m wheelchair
faux, f fausse wrong
félicitations ! congratulations!
féministe feminist
femme f woman; wife
femme de chambre f chambermaid
fenêtre f window
fer m iron
fer à repasser m iron
ferme f farm
fermé closed
fermer close; **fermer à clé** lock
fermeture éclair f zip
ferry-boat m ferry
fête f party
feu m fire; **vous avez du feu ?** have you got a light?
feuille f leaf
feux arrière mpl rear lights
feux d'artifice mpl fireworks
feux de position mpl sidelights
feux de signalisation mpl traffic lights
février February

fiancé m, **fiancée** f fiancé, f fiancée
fiancé engaged
ficelle f string
fier proud
fièvre f fever
fil m thread
fil de fer m wire
filet m fillet
fille f girl; daughter
film m film
filtre m filter
fin f end
fin fine
finir finish
flash m flash
fleur f flower
fleuriste m florist's
flirter flirt
foie m liver
foire f fair
fois f time; **une fois** once
fond m bottom; **au fond de** at the bottom of
fond de teint m foundation cream
fontaine f fountain
football m football
forêt f forest
forme f: **en forme** fit
formulaire m form
fort strong; loud
fou, f folle mad
foulard m scarf
foule f crowd
fouler: je me suis foulé la cheville I've sprained my ankle
four m oven
fourchette f fork
fourmi f ant
fracture f fracture

FRENCH-ENGLISH

frais, *f* **fraîche** fresh
fraise *f* strawberry
framboise *f* raspberry
français French
Français Frenchman; **une Française** a French woman; **les Français** the French
France *f* France
frapper hit
frein *m* brake
frein à main *m* handbrake
freiner brake
frère *m* brother
frigo *m* fridge
frire fry
frites *fpl* chips
froid cold
fromage *m* cheese
front *m* forehead
frontière *f* border
fruits *mpl* fruit
fruits de mer *mpl* seafood
fuite *f* leak
fumée *f* smoke
fumer smoke
fumeurs smoking
furieux furious
fusible *m* fuse
fusil *m* gun
futur *m* future

gagner win
galerie *f* roof rack
gallois Welsh
gants *mpl* gloves
garage *m* garage
garantie *f* guarantee
garçon *m* boy; waiter

garder keep
gare *f* station
garer: se garer park
gare routière *f* bus station
gas-oil *m* diesel
gâteau *m* cake; **petit gâteau** biscuit
gauche *f* left; **à gauche (de)** on the left (of)
gaucher left-handed
gaz *m* gas
gazeux fizzy
gel *m* frost
gênant embarrassing
genou *m* knee
gens *mpl* people
gibier *m* game
gilet *m* cardigan
gin *m* gin
gin-tonic *m* gin and tonic
gîte *m* self-catering flat/cottage
glace *f* ice; ice cream
glaçon *m* ice cube
glissant slippery
gomme *f* rubber
gorge *f* throat
goût *m* taste
goûter taste
goutte *f* drop
gouvernement *m* government
grammaire *f* grammar
grand large; tall
Grande-Bretagne *f* Great Britain
grand magasin *m* department store
grand-mère *f* grandmother
grand-père *m* grandfather
gras *m* fat
gras, *f* **grasse** greasy
gratuit free

FRENCH-ENGLISH

grec, *f* **grecque** Greek
Grèce *f* Greece
grêle *f* hail
grillé grilled
grippe *f* flu
gris grey
gros big; fat
grossier rude
grotte *f* cave
groupe *m* group
groupe sanguin *m* blood group
guêpe *f* wasp
guerre *f* war
gueule de bois *f* hangover
guichet *m* ticket office; box office
guide *m* guide
guitare *f* guitar

habiller dress; **s'habiller** dress
habiter live
habitude *f* habit
habituel usual
hache *f* axe
hamburger *m* hamburger
hanche *f* hip
handicapé disabled
haricots *mpl* beans; **haricots verts** green beans
hasard *m*: **par hasard** by chance
haut high
hélicoptère *m* helicopter
hémorroïdes *fpl* piles
herbe *f* grass; **des fines herbes** herbs

heure *f* hour; **quelle heure est-il ?** what time is it?; **5 heures du matin** 5 a.m.; **3 heures de l'après-midi** 3 p.m.; **11 heures du soir** 11 p.m.; **à l'heure** on time
heureusement fortunately
heureux happy
hier yesterday
histoire *f* history; story
hiver *m* winter
hobby *m* hobby
hollandais Dutch
Hollande *f* Holland
homard *m* lobster
homme *m* man
homosexuel gay
honnête honest
honteux ashamed
hôpital *m* hospital
hoquet *m* hiccups
horaire *m* timetable
horloge *f* clock
horrible horrible
hors-bord *m* motorboat
hors taxes duty-free
hospitalité *f* hospitality
hôtel *m* hotel
hôtesse de l'air *f* air hostess
huile *f* oil
huile d'olive *f* olive oil
huile solaire *f* suntan oil
huître *f* oyster
humeur *f* mood
humide damp
humour *m* humour

ici here

idée f idea
idiot m idiot
il he; **il y a trois jours** three days ago
île f island
ils they
immédiatement immediately
imperméable m raincoat
important important
impossible impossible
imprimé m printed matter
incroyable incredible
indépendant independent
indicatif m dialling code
indigestion f indigestion
industrie f industry
infection f infection
infirmière f nurse
innocent innocent
insecte m insect
insolation f sunstroke
insomnie f insomnia
instrument de musique m musical instrument
insupportable obnoxious
intelligent intelligent
interdit prohibited
intéressant interesting
intérieur m: **à l'intérieur** inside
interrupteur m switch
intoxication alimentaire f food poisoning
invitation f invitation
invité m guest
inviter invite
irlandais Irish
Irlande f Ireland
Irlande du Nord f Northern Ireland
Italie f Italy
italien Italian
itinéraire m route

ivre drunk

jaloux jealous
jamais never; **avez-vous jamais . . . ?** have you ever . . . ?
jambe f leg
jambon m ham
janvier January
jardin m garden
jauge f gauge
jaune yellow
jazz m jazz
je I
jean m jeans
jeter throw; throw away
jeu m game
jeudi Thursday
jeune young
jogging m jogging; **je fais du jogging** I go jogging
joli pretty
jouer play
jouet m toy
jour m day
jour férié m public holiday
journal m newspaper
journée f day
juif, f juïve Jewish
juillet July
juin June
jumeaux mpl twins
jupe f skirt
jus m juice
jusqu'à (ce que) until
juste fair; right

FRENCH-ENGLISH

kilo *m* kilo
kilomètre *m* kilometre
klaxon *m* horn
K-way *m* cagoule

la the; her
là there
là-bas over there; down there
lac *m* lake
lacets *mpl* shoe laces
là-haut up there
laid ugly
laine *f* wool
laisser let; leave
lait *m* milk
lait solaire *m* suntan lotion
laitue *f* lettuce
lame de rasoir *f* razor blade
lampe *f* lamp
lampe de poche *f* torch
lancer throw
landau *m* pram
langouste *f* crayfish
langoustine *f* crayfish
langue *f* tongue; language
lapin *m* rabbit
laque *f* hair spray
lard *m* bacon
large wide
lavabo *m* washbasin
laver wash; se laver wash
lave-vaisselle *m* dish washer
lavomatic *m* launderette

laxatif *m* laxative
le the; him
leçon *f* lesson
lecteur de cassettes *m* cassette player
léger light
légumes *mpl* vegetables
lent slow
lentement slowly
lentilles de contact *fpl* contact lenses
lentilles dures *fpl* hard lenses
lentilles semi-rigides *fpl* gas-permeable lenses
lentilles souples *fpl* soft lenses
les the; them
lessive *f* washing powder; faire la lessive do the washing
lettre *f* letter
leur their; them; le/la leur theirs
lever: se lever get up
levier de vitesses *m* gear lever
lèvre *f* lip
lézard *m* lizard
librairie *f* bookshop
libre free
lime à ongles *f* nailfile
limitation de vitesse *f* speed limit
limonade *f* lemonade
linge sale *m* laundry
liqueur *f* liqueur
lire read
liste *f* list
lit *m* bed; lit pour une personne/ deux personnes single/ double bed
lit de camp *m* campbed
lit d'enfant *m* cot

105

litre *m* litre
lits superposés *mpl* bunk beds
living *m* living room
livre *f* pound
livre *m* book
location de voitures *f* car rental
locomotive *f* engine
logement *m* accommodation
loger stay
loi *f* law
loin far; **plus loin** further
Londres London
long, f longue long
longtemps a long time
longueur *f* length
lorsque when
louer rent; **à louer** for hire
lourd heavy; rich
loyer *m* rent
lui him, *f* her
lumière *f* light
lundi Monday
lune *f* moon
lunettes *fpl* glasses
lunettes de soleil *fpl* sunglasses

M: M Dumas Mr Dumas
ma my
machine à écrire *f* typewriter
machine à laver *f* washing machine
macho macho
mâchoire *f* jaw
madame Madam

Mademoiselle Miss
magasin *m* shop
magazine *m* magazine
magnétoscope *m* video recorder
mai May
maigre skinny
maillot de bain *m* swimming costume
main *f* hand
maintenant now
mairie *f* town hall
mais but
maison *f* house; **à la maison** at home; **fait maison** homemade
mal *m*: **j'ai mal ici** I have a pain here; **j'ai mal à la tête/ gorge** I've got a headache/ sore throat; **ça fait mal** it hurts
mal badly; **je me sens mal** I feel sick
malade ill
maladie *f* disease
maladie vénérienne *f* VD
mal de mer *m*: **j'ai le mal de mer** I'm seasick
mal du pays *m*: **j'ai le mal du pays** I'm homesick
malentendu *m* misunderstanding
malheureusement unfortunately
maman *f* mum
Manche *f* Channel
manger eat
manquer: tu me manques I miss you
manteau *m* coat
manuel de conversation *m* phrase book
maquillage *m* make-up

marchand de légumes m greengrocer

marchand de vins m off-licence

marché m market

marche arrière f reverse gear

marcher walk; **ça ne marche pas** it's not working

mardi Tuesday

marée f tide

margarine f margarine

mari m husband

mariage m wedding

marié married

marre: j'en ai marre (de) I'm fed up (with)

marron m chestnut

marron brown

mars March

marteau m hammer

mascara m mascara

match m match

matelas m mattress

matin m morning

mauvais bad

maux d'estomac mpl stomach ache

mayonnaise f mayonnaise

me me; myself

mécanicien m mechanic

médecin m doctor

médicament m medicine

Méditerranée f Mediterranean

méduse f jellyfish

meilleur: le meilleur the best; **meilleur que** better than

mélanger mix

melon m melon

même same; **même les hommes/ si** even men/ if; **moi/ lui-même** myself, himself

mentir lie

menton m chin

menu m set menu

mer f sea

merci thank you

mercredi Wednesday

mère f mother

merveilleux wonderful

mes my

message m message

messe f mass

métal m metal

météo f weather forecast

métier m job

mètre m meter

métro m underground

mettre put

meubles mpl furniture

midi midday

miel m honey

mien: le mien, la mienne mine

mieux better

milieu m middle

mince thin

minuit midnight

minute f minute

miroir m mirror

Mlle Miss, Ms

Mme Mrs, Ms

mobylette f moped

mode f fashion; **à la mode** fashionable

moderne modern

moi me

moins less; **au moins** at least

mois m month

moitié f half

mon my

monde m world; **tout le monde** everyone

moniteur *m*, **monitrice** *f* instructor
monnaie *f* change
monsieur *m* gentleman; **Monsieur** sir
montagne *f* mountain
monter go up; get in
montre *f* watch
montrer show
monument *m* monument
moquette *f* carpet
morceau *m* piece
morsure *f* bite
mort *f* death
mort dead
mot *m* word
moteur *m* engine
moto *f* motorbike
mouche *f* fly
mouchoir *m* handkerchief
mouette *f* seagull
mouillé wet
moules *fpl* mussels
mourir die
mousse à raser *f* shaving foam
moustache *f* moustache
moustique *m* mosquito
moutarde *f* mustard
mouton *m* sheep; mutton
moyen âge *m* Middle Ages
mur *m* wall
mûr ripe
mûre *f* blackberry
muscle *m* muscle
musée *m* museum; **musée d'art** art gallery
musique *f* music; **musique classique/ folklorique/ pop** classical/ folk/ pop music
myope shortsighted

nager swim
naître: je suis né en 1963 I was born in 1963
nappe *f* tablecloth
natation *f* swimming
nationalité *f* nationality
nature *f* nature
naturel natural
nécessaire necessary
négatif *m* negative
neige *f* snow
nerveux nervous
nettoyer clean
neuf, f neuve new
neveu *m* nephew
névrosé neurotic
nez *m* nose
ni ... ni ... neither ... nor ...
nièce *f* niece
Noël Christmas
noir black
noir et blanc black and white
noisette *f* hazelnut
noix *f* walnut
nom *m* name
nom de famille *m* surname
nom de jeune fille *m* maiden name
non no
non-fumeurs non-smoking
nord *m* north; **au nord de** north of
normal normal
nos our
note *f* bill
notre our
nôtre: le/la nôtre ours
nourriture *f* food

nous we; us
nouveau, f **nouvelle** new; **de nouveau** again
Nouvel An m New Year
nouvelles fpl news
novembre November
nu naked
nuage m cloud
nuageux cloudy
nuit f night; **bonne nuit** good night
nulle part nowhere
numéro m number
numéro de téléphone m phone number

objectif m lens
objets trouvés mpl lost property office
obtenir get
obturateur m shutter
occasion f: **d'occasion** second-hand
occupé engaged; busy
occuper: s'occuper de take care of
octobre October
odeur f smell
oeil m, pl **yeux** eye
oeuf m egg; **oeuf dur/ à la coque** hard-boiled/ boiled egg; **oeufs brouillés** scrambled eggs
offrir offer; give
oie f goose
oignon m onion
oiseau m bird
olive f olive

ombre f shade
ombre à paupières f eye shadow
omelette f omelette
on one; you; we; **on dit que** they say that; **on vous demande** someone is asking for you
oncle m uncle
ongle m fingernail
opéra m opera
opération f operation
opticien m optician
optimiste optimistic
or m gold
orage m thunderstorm
orange f orange
orange orange
orchestre m orchestra
ordinateur m computer
ordonnance f prescription
ordures fpl litter
oreille f ear
oreiller m pillow
organiser organize
orteil m toe
os m bone
oser dare
ou or
où where
oublier forget
ouest m west; **à l'ouest de** west of
oui yes
outil m tool
ouvert open
ouvre-boîte m tin-opener
ouvre-bouteille m bottle-opener
ouvrir open

P

pagaille f mess
page f page
pain m bread; **pain blanc/ complet** white/ wholemeal bread
paire f pair
palais m palace
pamplemousse m grapefruit
panier m basket
panique f panic
panne f breakdown; **tomber en panne** break down
panneau de signalisation m roadsign
pansement m bandage
pansement adhésif m Elastoplast (R)
pantalon m trousers
pantoufles fpl slippers
papa m dad
papeterie f stationer's
papier m paper
papier à lettres m writing paper
papier collant m sellotape (R)
papier d'aluminium m silver foil
papier d'emballage m wrapping paper
papier hygiénique m toilet paper
papillon m butterfly
Pâques Easter
paquet m package; packet
par by; through; **par semaine** per week
parapluie m umbrella
parc m park
parce que because

pardon excuse me
pare-brise m windscreen
pare-chocs m bumper
parents mpl relatives; parents
paresseux lazy
parfait perfect
parfois sometimes
parfum m perfume
parking m car park
parler speak
parmi among
partager share
partie f part
partir leave
partout everywhere
pas not; **je ne suis pas fatigué** I'm not tired; **pas de … no …**
passage à niveau m level crossing
passage clouté m pedestrian crossing
passager m passenger
passeport m passport
passionnant exciting
pastilles pour la gorge fpl throat pastilles
pâté m pâté
pâtes fpl pasta
pâtisserie f cake; cake shop
patron m manager
pauvre poor
payer pay
pays m country
paysage m scenery
Pays de Galles m Wales
PCV m reverse charge call
peau f skin
pêche f peach; fishing
pédale f pedal
peigne m comb
peindre paint
pelle f spade

pellicule f film
pelouse f lawn
pendant during; **pendant que** while
pénicilline f penicillin
pénis m penis
penser think
pension f guesthouse
pension complète f full board
perdre lose
père m father
permanente f perm
permettre allow
permis allowed
permis de conduire m driving licence
personne f person
personne nobody
petit small
petit déjeuner m breakfast
petit pain m roll
petits pois mpl peas
peu: peu de touristes few tourists; **un peu (de)** a little bit (of)
peur f fear; **j'ai peur (de)** I'm afraid (of)
peut-être maybe
phallocrate m male chauvinist pig
phare m lighthouse
phares mpl headlights
pharmacie f chemist's
photographe m photographer
photographie f photograph
photographier photograph
photomètre m light meter
pickpocket m pickpocket
picnic m picnic
pièce de théâtre f play
pièces de rechange fpl spare parts

pied m foot; **à pied** on foot
pierre f stone
piéton m pedestrian
pile f battery
pilote m pilot
pilule f pill
pince f pliers
pince à épiler f tweezers
pince à linge f clothes peg
pince à ongles f nail clippers
pinceau m paint brush
ping-pong m table tennis
pipe f pipe
piquant hot
piquer sting
piqûre f injection; bite
pire worse; **le/la pire** the worst
piscine f swimming pool
place f seat; square
plafond m ceiling
plage f beach
plaindre: se plaindre (de) complain (about)
plaisanterie f joke
plan m plan; map
planche à voile f sailboard
plancher m floor
plante f plant
plaque minéralogique f number plate
plastique m plastic
plat flat
plat m dish
plateau m tray
plein full
pleurer cry
pleuvoir rain; **il pleut** it's raining
plombage m filling
plombier m plumber
plongée sous-marine f skindiving

plonger dive
pluie f rain
plupart f: **la plupart de** most of
plus more; **plus de ...** no more ...
plusieurs several
plutôt rather
pneu m tyre
pneu de rechange m spare tyre
pneumonie f pneumonia
poche f pocket
poêle f frying pan
poids m weight
poignée f handle
poignet m wrist
poire f pear
poireau m leek
poison m poison
poisson m fish
poissonnerie f fishmonger's
poitrine f chest
poivre m pepper (spice)
poivron m pepper
poli polite
police f police
politique f politics
politique political
pollué polluted
pommade f ointment
pomme f apple
pomme de terre f potato
pompiers mpl fire brigade
poney m pony
pont m bridge; deck
porc m pork
port m harbour
porte f door; gate
porte-bébé m carry-cot
portefeuille m wallet
porte-monnaie m purse
porter carry

portier m porter
portion f portion
porto m port
possible possible
poste f post office
poster m poster
poster post
poste restante f poste restante
pot m jug
potage m soup
pot d'échappement m exhaust
poubelle f dustbin
poule f chicken
poulet m chicken
poulpe m octopus
poumons mpl lungs
poupée f doll
pour for
pourboire m tip
pour cent per cent
pourquoi why
pourri rotten
pousser push
poussette f pushchair
pouvoir: je peux/ il peut I/ he can
pratique practical
prêter lend
préféré favourite
préférer prefer
premier first
premier m first floor
première f first class
premiers secours mpl first aid
prendre take
prénom m first name
préparer prepare
près de near
présenter introduce
préservatif m condom
presque almost

FRENCH-ENGLISH

pressing *m* dry-cleaner's
prêt ready
prêtre *m* priest
prince *m* prince
princesse *f* princess
principal main
printemps *m* spring
priorité *f* right of way
prise *f* plug; socket
prise multiple *f* adaptor
prison *f* prison
privé private
prix *m* price
probablement probably
problème *m* problem
prochain next; **l'année
prochaine** next year
produits de beauté *mpl*
cosmetics
professeur *m* teacher
profond deep
programme *m* programme
promenade *f* walk
promener: aller se promener
go for a walk
promettre promise
prononcer pronounce
propre clean; **sa propre clef**
his/her own key
propriétaire *m* owner
prospectus *m* brochure
protège-couches *mpl* nappy-
liners
protéger protect
protestant Protestant
prudent careful
prune *f* plum
public public
public *m* public; audience
puce *f* flea
puis then
pull(over) *m* sweater
punk punk

pyjama *m* pyjamas

quai *m* platform; quay
qualité *f* quality
quand when
quand-même anyway
quart *m* quarter
quartier *m* district
que: plus laid que uglier
than; **je pense que . . .** I
think that . . .; **que . . . ?**
what . . .? **je ne fume que . . .**
I only smoke . . .
quel which
quelque chose something
quelque part somewhere
quelques-uns some
quelqu'un somebody
queue *f* tail; queue; **faire la
queue** queue
qui who
quincaillerie *f* ironmonger's
quinzaine *f* fortnight
quoi ? what?

raccourci *m* shortcut
radiateur *m* heater; radiator
radio *f* radio; X-ray
raide steep
raisin *m* grapes
raisonnable sensible
rallonge *f* extension lead

113

rapide fast
rare rare
raser: se raser shave
rasoir *m* razor
rat *m* rat
rater miss
ravissant lovely
rayon *m* spoke
rayons X *mpl* X-ray
réception *f* reception
réceptionniste *m/f* receptionist
recette *f* recipe
receveur *m* conductor
recevoir receive
recommander recommend
reconnaissant grateful
reconnaître recognize
reçu *m* receipt
regarder look (at)
régime *m* diet
région *f* area
règles *fpl* period
rein *m* kidney
reine *f* queen
religion *f* religion
rembourser refund
remercier thank
remorque *f* trailer
remplir fill
rencontrer meet
rendez-vous *m* appointment
rendre give back
renseignement *m* information
renseignements *mpl* information desk; directory enquiries
rentrer return; **rentrer à la maison** go home
renverser knock over
réparer repair
repas *m* meal

repasser iron
répéter repeat
répondre answer
réponse *f* answer
reposer: se reposer take a rest
représentant *m* agent
réservation *f* reservation
réserver book
réservoir *m* tank
respirer breathe
responsable responsible
ressembler à look like
ressort *m* spring
restaurant *m* restaurant
reste *m* rest
rester stay
retard *m* delay; **en retard** late
retraité *m* old-age pensioner
rétroviseur *m* rearview mirror
réunion *f* meeting
rêve *m* dream
réveil *m* alarm clock
réveillé awake
réveiller wake up; **se réveiller** wake up
revenir come back
rez-de-chaussée *m* ground floor
rhum *m* rum
rhumatismes *mpl* rheumatism
rhume *m* cold
rhume des foins *m* hay fever
riche rich
rideau *m* curtain
ridicule ridiculous
rien nothing; anything
rire laugh
rivage *m* shore
rivière *f* river
riz *m* rice

robe *f* dress
robe de chambre *f* dressing gown
robinet *m* tap
rocher *m* rock
rock *m* rock music
roi *m* king
roman *m* novel
rond round
rond-point *m* roundabout
ronfler snore
rose pink
rose *f* rose
rosé *m* rosé wine
roue *f* wheel
rouge red
rouge à lèvres *m* lipstick
rougeole *f* measles
route *f* road
roux, *f* rousse red-headed
rubéole *f* German measles
rue *f* street
ruines *fpl* ruins
ruisseau *m* stream

sa his, her, its
sable *m* sand
sac *m* bag; **sac en plastique** plastic bag
sac à dos *m* rucksack
sac à main *m* handbag
sac de couchage *m* sleeping bag
saigner bleed
saison *f* season; **en haute saison** in the high season
salade *f* salad
sale dirty

salé salty
salle à manger *f* dining room
salle d'attente *f* waiting room
salle de bain *f* bathroom
salon *m* lounge
samedi Saturday
sandales *fpl* sandals
sandwich *m* sandwich
sang *m* blood
sans without
santé *f* health; **bon pour la santé** healthy; **santé !** your health!; bless you!
sardine *f* sardine
sauce *f* sauce
saucisse *f* sausage
sauf except
saumon *m* salmon
sauna *m* sauna
sauter jump
sauvage wild
savoir know; **je ne sais pas** I don't know
savon *m* soap
scandaleux shocking
Scandinavie *f* Scandinavia
science *f* science
seau *m* bucket
sec, *f* sèche dry
sèche-cheveux *m* hair dryer
sécher dry
seconde *f* second; second class
secret secret
sécurité *f*: **en sécurité** safe
séduisant attractive
sein *m* breast
séjour *m* stay
sel *m* salt
self-service self-service
sels de bain *mpl* bath salts
semaine *f* week
semblable similar

semelle *f* sole
sens *m* direction
sensible sensitive
sentier *m* path
sentiment *m* feeling
sentir feel; smell; **je me sens bien/ mal** I feel well/ unwell
séparé separate
séparément separately
septembre September
sérieux serious
serpent *m* snake
serrure *f* lock
serveuse *f* waitress
service *m* service; service charge
serviette *f* briefcase; serviette
serviette de bain *f* towel
serviette hygiénique *f* sanitary towel
servir serve
ses his, her, its
seul alone
seulement only
sexe *m* sex
sexiste sexist
sexy sexy
shampoing *m* shampoo
shopping *m* shopping; **faire du shopping** go shopping
shorts *mpl* shorts
si if; so; yes
SIDA *m* AIDS
siècle *m* century
siège *m* seat
sien: le sien, la sienne his, hers
signer sign
signifier mean
silence *m* silence; **silence !** quiet!
s'il vous plaît please

simple simple
sincère sincere
sinon otherwise
ski *m* ski; skiing
skier ski
ski nautique *m* waterski; waterskiing
slip *m* underpants
slip de bain *m* swimming trunks
société *f* company; **la Société** society
soeur *f* sister
soie *f* silk
soif *f*: **j'ai soif** I'm thirsty
soir *m* evening; **ce soir** tonight
soirée *f* evening
soit ... soit ... either ... or ...
soldes *mpl* sale
soleil *m* sun
sombre dark
sommeil *m*: **j'ai sommeil** I'm sleepy
somnifère *m* sleeping pill
son his, her, its
sonnette *f* bell
sortie *f* exit
sortie de secours *f* emergency exit
sortir go out
souci *m* worry; **se faire du souci (pour)** worry (about)
soucoupe *f* saucer
soudain suddenly
soupe *f* soup
sourcil *m* eyebrow
sourd deaf
sourire smile
souris *f* mouse
sous under
sous-sol *m* basement

FRENCH-ENGLISH

sous-vêtements *mpl* underwear
soutien-gorge *m* bra
souvenir *m* souvenir
souvenir: se souvenir de remember
souvent often
spécialement especially
spécialité *f* speciality
sport *m* sport
starter *m* choke
stationner park
station-service *f* petrol station
steak *m* steak
stérilet *m* IUD
steward *m* steward
studio *m* flatlet
stupide stupid
stylo *m* pen
stylo à bille *m* biro (R)
stylo-feutre *m* felt-tip pen
succès *m* success
sucette *f* lollipop
sucre *m* sugar
sucré sweet
sud *m* south; **au sud de** south of
suffire: ça suffit that's enough
Suisse *f* Switzerland; **Suisse romande** French-speaking Switzerland
suisse Swiss
suivant next
suivre follow; **faire suivre** forward
super tremendous
supermarché *m* supermarket
supplément *m* supplement
supporter: je ne supporte pas le fromage I can't stand cheese

sur on
sûr sure
surf *m* surf
surgelé frozen; **les surgelés** frozen food
surnom *m* nickname
surprenant surprising
surprise *f* surprise
survêtement de sport *m* tracksuit
sympathique nice
synagogue *f* synagogue

ta your
tabac *m* tobacco
tabac-journaux *m* newsagent
table *f* table
tableau *m* painting
tableau de bord *m* dashboard
tache *f* stain
taille *f* size; waist
taille-crayon *m* pencil sharpener
talc *m* talcum powder
talon *m* heel
tampon *m* tampon
tante *f* aunt
tapis *m* rug
tard late
tarte *f* tart; **tarte aux pommes** apple pie
tasse *f* cup
taureau *m* bull
taxi *m* taxi
te you
teinturier *m* dry-cleaner's
téléférique *m* cable car
télégramme *m* telemessage

téléphone *m* telephone
téléphoner (à) phone
télésiège *m* chairlift
télévision *f* television
témoin *m* witness
température *f* temperature
tempête *f* storm
temple *m* Protestant church
temps *m* time; weather
tenir hold
tennis *m* tennis
tennis *fpl* trainers
tente *f* tent
terminer finish
terrain pour caravanes *m* caravan site
terre *f* earth
tes your
tête *f* head
thé *m* tea
théâtre *m* theatre
théière *f* teapot
thermomètre *m* thermometer
thermos *m* thermos flask
thon *m* tuna fish
tiède lukewarm
tien: le tien, la tienne yours
timbre *m* stamp
timide shy
tire-bouchon *m* corkscrew
tirer pull
tissu *m* material
toast *m* toast
toi you
toilettes *fpl* toilet
toit *m* roof
tomate *f* tomato
tomber fall; **laisser tomber** drop
ton your
tonnerre *m* thunder
torchon à vaisselle *m* tea towel

tôt early
toucher touch
toujours always; still
tour *f* tower
touriste *m* tourist
tourner turn
tournevis *m* screwdriver
tous, *f* **toutes** all; **tous les deux** both of them; **tous les jours** every day
tousser cough
tout everything; **tout le/ toute la** all the; **toute la journée** all day; **en tout** altogether
toutes all
toux *f* cough
tradition *f* tradition
traditionnel traditional
traduire translate
train *m* train
tranche *f* slice
tranquille quiet
transmission *f* transmission
transpirer sweat
travail *m* work
travailler work
travaux *mpl* roadworks
traverser cross
très very
tricoter knit
triste sad
trop too much; **trop cher/vite** too expensive/ fast
trottoir *m* pavement
trou *m* hole
trouver find
T-shirt *m* T-shirt
tu you
tuer kill
tunnel *m* tunnel
tuyau *m* pipe

FRENCH-ENGLISH

un, *f* **une** a, an; one
université *f* university
urgence *f* emergency
urgent urgent
usine *f* factory
ustensiles de cuisine *mpl*
  cooking utensils
utile useful
utiliser use

vacances *fpl* holiday;
  grandes vacances summer
  holidays
vaccin *m* vaccination
vache *f* cow
vagin *m* vagina
vague *f* wave
vaisselle *f* crockery; **faire la**
  vaisselle do the washing
  up
valable valid
valise *f* suitcase
vallée *f* valley
vanille *f* vanilla
varappe *f* rock climbing
variable changeable
vase *m* vase
veau *m* veal
végétarien vegetarian
véhicule *m* vehicle
vélo *m* bicycle
vendre sell
vendredi Friday
venir come

vent *m* wind
vente *f* sale
ventilateur *m* fan
ventre *m* stomach
vérifier check
vernis à ongles *m* nail polish
verre *m* glass
verrou *m* bolt
verrouiller bolt
vert green
vessie *f* bladder
veste *f* jacket
vestiaire *m* cloakroom
vêtements *mpl* clothes
vétérinaire *m* vet
veuf *m* widower
veuve *f* widow
vexer offend
viande *f* meat
viande hachée *f* minced meat
vide empty
vidéo *f* video
vie *f* life
vieux, *f* **vieille** old
vignoble *m* vineyard
vilebrequin *m* crankshaft
villa *f* villa
village *m* village
ville *f* town
vin *m* wine; **vin rouge/**
  blanc/ rosé red/ white/ rosé
  wine
vinaigre *m* vinegar
vinaigrette *f* salad dressing
viol *m* rape
violet purple
virage *m* bend
vis *f* screw
visa *m* visa
visage *m* face
viseur *m* viewfinder
visite *f* visit
visiter visit

FRENCH-ENGLISH

vitamines *fpl* vitamins
vite quickly
vitesse *f* speed; gear
vivant alive
vivre live
voeux *mpl:* **meilleurs voeux**
best wishes
voici here is/are
voilà here is/are
voile *f* sail; sailing
voir see
voisin *m*, **voisine** *f*
neighbour
voiture *f* car
voix *f* voice
vol *m* flight; theft
volaille *f* poultry
volant *m* steering wheel
voler steal; fly
volets *mpl* shutters
voleur *m* thief
vomir: j'ai envie de vomir
I'm going to be sick
vos your
votre your
vôtre: le/la vôtre yours
vouloir want; **je veux** I
want; **voulez-vous . . . ?** do
you want . . . ?
vous you
voyage *m* trip; **voyage**
d'affaires business trip;
bon voyage ! have a good
journey!
voyage de noces *m*
honeymoon
voyage organisé *m* package
tour
voyager travel
vrai true
vraiment really
vue *f* view

wagon *m* carriage
wagon-lit *m* sleeper
wagon-restaurant *m* dining
car
walkman *m* (R) walkman (R)
WC *mpl* toilet
week-end *m* weekend

y there; **il y a** there is/are
yacht *m* yacht
yaourt *m* yoghurt
yeux *mpl* eyes

zéro zero
zone piétonne *f* pedestrian
precinct
zoo *m* zoo

GRAMMAR

French has two *GENDERS*, masculine (*m*) and feminine (*f*). For masculine nouns the definite article (the) is **le** (or **l'** before a word beginning with a vowel or an 'h' that is not pronounced) and the indefinite article (a, an) is **un**:

le journal	the newspaper
l'homme	the man
un journal	a newspaper
un homme	a man

For feminine nouns the word for 'the' is **la** (or **l'** before a word beginning with a vowel or with an 'h' that is not pronounced) and the word for 'a' is **une**:

la femme	the woman
l'addition	the bill
une femme	a woman
une addition	a bill

The plural for both genders for the definite article (the) is **les**:

les hommes	the men
les femmes	the women

The plural for the indefinite article (eg some) is **des**:

des hommes	(some) men
des femmes	(some) women

When used with the common words **à** (to, at) and **de** (of, from) the words **le**, **la** and **les** undergo certain changes:

à + le = au	**de + le = du**
à + les = aux	**de + les = des**

au cinéma
at/to the cinema

aux Tuileries, s'il vous plaît
to the Tuileries please

le nom du café
the name of the café

la télévision des voisins
the neighbours' television

121

GRAMMAR

No change is made with **la** or **l'**:

je vais à la plage	I'm going to the beach
le nom de l'hôtel	the name of the hotel

The *PLURALS* of nouns are generally formed by adding an **-s** (although this is not pronounced):

le café	the café
les cafés	the cafés

If the singular noun ends in **-au**, **-eau**, **-eu** or **-ou** then the plural is formed by adding an **-x** (again this is not pronounced):

le bateau	the boat
les bateaux	the boats
le feu	the fire
les feux	the fires

If the singular ends in **-x** then there is no change in the plural:

le prix	the price
les prix	the prices

If the singular noun ends in **-al** then the plural is formed by changing **-al** to **-aux**:

le journal	the newspaper
les journaux	the newspapers

Most *ADJECTIVES* in French come after the noun:

le manteau vert	the green coat

But some common adjectives come before the noun:

beau	beautiful	**grand**	big
bon	good	**mauvais**	bad
gentil	nice	**petit**	little
jeune	young	**vieux**	old
joli	pretty		

Adjectives in French must agree with their noun. This means that if a noun is feminine then the adjective must be feminine too; if the noun is plural then the adjective must be plural too. To form the feminine of most adjectives you simply add **-e**:

une voiture verte	a green car

To form the plural use the same rules as for nouns:

des touristes anglaises	some English (women) tourists

GRAMMAR

There are some special feminine endings:

m	f	m	f
-as	-asse	-eur	-euse
-eil	-eille	-eux	-euse
-el	-elle	-f	-ve
-en	-enne	-on	-onne
-er	-ère	-os	-osse
-et	-ette or -ète		

Some adjectives have irregular feminines. These are shown in the dictionary section.

To form a *COMPARATIVE* put **plus** in front of the adjective:

| **grand** | big |
| **plus grand** | bigger |

'than' is **que**:

c'est plus grand que le mien
it's bigger than mine

'less' is **moins**:

c'est moins cher que le mien
it's less expensive than mine

'as . . . as' is **aussi . . . que**

aussi cher que le mien
as expensive as mine

SUPERLATIVES are formed with **le/la/les plus**:

le train le plus rapide   the fastest train

ADVERBS are formed by adding **-ment** to the feminine adjective:

nerveux   nervous   **nerveusement** nervously

POSSESSIVE ADJECTIVES agree with the thing that is possessed not the sex of the person etc that possesses. For example:

| **sa maison** | his/her house |
| **mon vélo** | my bike (said by both man and woman) |

	m	f	pl
my	**mon**	**ma**	**mes**
your (fam)*	**ton**	**ta**	**tes**
his/her/its	**son**	**sa**	**ses**
our	**notre**	**notre**	**nos**
your	**votre**	**votre**	**vos**
their	**leur**	**leur**	**leurs**

* familiar form if using **tu** for 'you'.

GRAMMAR

PERSONAL PRONOUNS

subject		object		indirect object	
je	I	me	me	me	to me
tu	you (fam)	te	you	te	to you
il	he/it	le	him/it	lui	to him/it
elle	she/it	la	her/it	lui	to her/it
nous	we	nous	us	nous	to us
vous	you	vous	you	vous	to you
ils	they (*m*)	les	them	leur	to them
elles	they (*f*)	les	them	leur	to them

Personal pronouns normally come before the verb:

je le/la connais	I know him/her
je lui ai parlé	I spoke to him/her

Other pronouns used for emphasis or after prepositions are:

moi	me	nous	us
toi	you	vous	you
lui	him	eux	them
elle	her	elles	them

c'est pour moi/elle	it's for me/her
venez avec moi/nous	come with me/us
qui ? – toi	who? – you
lui, il est ...	him, he's ...

There are two words for *YOU* in French. **Tu** (and its forms **te, toi**) are used to friends, relatives or children. **Vous** is used for someone you don't know as a friend.

With *REFLEXIVE* verbs like **se lever, s'appeler** use the following pronouns:

je me ...	nous nous ...
tu te ...	vous vous ...
il/elle se ...	ils/elles se ...

elle s'appelle Marie	she's called Marie
nous nous levons à ...	we get up at ...

GRAMMAR

POSSESSIVE PRONOUNS (like adjectives) agree with the object possessed:

	m sing	*f sing*	*m pl*	*f pl*
mine	le mien	la mienne	les miens	les miennes
yours	le tien	la tienne	les tiens	les tiennes
his/hers	le sien	la sienne	les siens	les siennes
ours	le nôtre	la nôtre	les nôtres	les nôtres
yours	le vôtre	la vôtre	les vôtres	les vôtres
theirs	le leur	la leur	les leurs	les leurs

ce n'est pas ton verre — c'est le mien
it's not your glass — it's mine

tu as ta clé ? — j'ai perdu la mienne
have you got your key? — I've lost mine

Note that you can also use the word **à** with one of the pronouns as listed above (pronouns used after prepositions):

c'est à moi/lui   it's mine/his

VERBS fall into three main groups with endings in **-er, -ir** and **-re**. The *PRESENT TENSE* (I speak, he finishes, they sell etc) is formed as follows:

		parler	finir	vendre
		(to speak)	(to finish)	(to sell)
I	je	parle	finis	vends
you	tu	parles	finis	vends
he/she/it	il/elle	parle	finit	vend
we	nous	parlons	finissons	vendons
you	vous	parlez	finissez	vendez
they	ils/elles	parlent	finissent	vendent

Note that the **-s** and **-ent** endings are not pronounced.

Two very useful **-ir** verbs are different:

partir (to leave)	sortir (to go out)
je pars	je sors
tu pars	tu sors
il/elle part	il/elle sort
nous partons	nous sortons
vous partez	vous sortez
ils/elles partent	ils/elles sortent

GRAMMAR

Some important verbs are irregular:

	être	avoir	faire	aller
	(to be)	(to have)	(to do/make)	(to go)
je	suis	j'ai	fais	vais
tu	es	as	fais	vas
il/elle	est	a	fait	va
nous	sommes	avons	faisons	allons
vous	êtes	avez	faites	allez
ils/ elles	sont	ont	font	vont

The *IMPERFECT* of the verbs 'to be' and 'to have' (I was, you were etc; I had, you had etc) is formed as follows:

être	avoir
j'étais	j'avais
tu étais	tu avais
il/elle était	il/elle avait
nous étions	nous avions
vous étiez	vous aviez
ils/elles étaient	ils/elles avaient

The *PAST TENSE* of most verbs is formed by adding the appropriate part of the verb **avoir** (to have) to the *PAST PARTICIPLE*:

parler (to speak)
j'ai parlé   I have spoken, I spoke
tu as parlé   you have spoken, you spoke
etc   etc

finir (to finish)
il a fini   he (has) finished
nous avons fini   we (have) finished

vendre (to sell)
vous avez vendu   you (have) sold
elles ont vendu   they (have) sold

Some important verbs use **être** not **avoir** (these are often verbs expressing motion):

je suis allé   I have gone, I went
tu es venu   you have come, you came
il est arrivé   he has arrived, he arrived
nous sommes rentrés   we have come back, we came back

vous êtes partis   you (have) left
elles sont sorties   they have gone out, they went out

GRAMMAR

Some common verbs have irregular past participles:

avoir (to have)	**eu** (had)
comprendre (to understand)	**compris** (understood)
dire (to say)	**dit** (said)
être (to be)	**été** (been)
faire (to make, to do)	**fait** (made, done)
mettre (to put)	**mis** (put)
voir (to see)	**vu** (seen)

The *FUTURE* (I will etc) is formed as follows:

	parler	finir	vendre
je	parlerai	finirai	vendrai
tu	parleras	finiras	vendras
il/elle	parlera	finira	vendra
nous	parlerons	finirons	vendrons
vous	parlerez	finirez	vendrez
ils/elles	parleront	finiront	vendront

être
je serai I will be
tu seras you will be
il/elle sera he/she will be

nous serons we will be
vous serez you will be
ils/elles seront they will be

avoir
j'aurai I will have
tu auras you will have
il/elle aura he/she will have

nous aurons we will have
vous aurez you will have
ils/elles auront they will have

CONVERSION TABLES

metres
  1 metre = 39.37 inches or 1.09 yards

kilometres
  1 kilometre = 0.62 or approximately ⅝ mile

to convert kilometres to miles: divide by 8 and multiply by 5

kilometres:	2	3	4	5	10	100
miles:	1.25	1.9	2.5	3.1	6.25	62.5

miles
to convert miles to kilometres: divide by 5 and multiply by 8

miles:	1	3	5	10	20	100
kilometres:	1.6	4.8	8	16	32	160

kilos
  1 kilo = 2.2 or approximately 11⅕ pounds

to convert kilos to pounds: divide by 5 and multiply by 11

kilos:	4	5	10	20	30	40
pounds:	8.8	11	22	44	66	88

pounds
  1 pound = 0.45 or approximately ⁵⁄₁₁ kilo

litres
  1 litre = approximately 1¾ pints or 0.22 gallons

Celsius
to convert to Fahrenheit: divide by 5, multiply by 9, add 32

Celsius:	10	15	20	25	28	30	34
Fahrenheit:	50	59	68	77	82	86	93

Fahrenheit
to convert Fahrenheit to Celsius: subtract 32, multiply by 5, divide by 9